PUBLIC HEALTH IN THE 21ST CENTURY

NATIONAL VACCINE INJURY COMPENSATION PROGRAM

PROVISIONS AND ISSUES

PUBLIC HEALTH IN THE 21ST CENTURY

Additional books in this series can be found on Nova's website
under the Series tab.

Additional e-books in this series can be found on Nova's website
under the e-book tab.

PUBLIC HEALTH IN THE 21ST CENTURY

NATIONAL VACCINE INJURY COMPENSATION PROGRAM

PROVISIONS AND ISSUES

PRESTON TORRES
EDITOR

NOVINKA

New York

NOTICE TO THE READER

Library of Congress Cataloging-in-Publication Data

ISBN: 978-1-63482-528-3

Published by Nova Science Publishers, Inc. † New York

CONTENTS

Preface **vii**

Chapter 1 Vaccine Injury Compensation: Most Claims Took Multiple Years and Many Were Settled through Negotiation **1**
United States Government Accountability Office

Chapter 2 What You Need to Know About the National Vaccine Injury Compensation Program **39**
Health Resources and Services Administration

Chapter 3 National Vaccine Injury Compensation Program Statistics Report **55**
Health Resources and Services Administration

Chapter 4 The National Childhood Vaccine Injury Act and Preemption: An Overview of *Bruesewitz v. Wyeth* **65**
Vivian S. Chu

Index **87**

PREFACE

This book examines how long it has taken to adjudicate claims and how claims have been adjudicated; the changes to the vaccine injury table; and how the balance of and spending from the Vaccine Injury Compensation Trust Fund have changed, among other objectives.

Chapter 1 – Vaccines save lives by preventing disease in the people who receive them. In some instances, however, a vaccine can have severe side effects, including death or an injury requiring lifetime medical care. VICP provides compensation to people for injuries and deaths associated with certain vaccines for medical and other costs. The program includes an injury table that lists the injuries that are presumed to be caused by vaccines covered by the program. The program may also compensate individuals for injuries not on the table; however, in those cases causation is not presumed. In both cases, medical and other records are required. VICP pays claims from a trust fund. Since the program began in 1988, it has awarded more than $2.8 billion in compensation.

GAO was asked to review the program. GAO examined (1) how long it has taken to adjudicate claims and how claims have been adjudicated, (2) the changes to the vaccine injury table, and (3) how the balance of and spending from the Vaccine Injury Compensation Trust Fund have changed, among other objectives.

GAO examined data and interviewed officials from HHS, DOJ, and USCFC, including data on claims filed since fiscal year 1999 and their status as of March 31, 2014; reviewed laws and agency documents; and reviewed Treasury data and agency data on compensation and obligations for other VICP-related expenses for fiscal years 2009 through 2013.

HHS and USCFC agreed with GAO's findings, and HHS, USCFC, DOJ, and Treasury provided technical comments that were incorporated as appropriate.

Chapter 2 – Vaccines save lives by preventing disease in the people who receive them. Most people who get vaccines have no serious problems. However, vaccines, like any medicines, can rarely cause serious problems, such as severe allergic reactions. In those rare cases, the VICP, which is a Federal program, provides compensation to people found to be injured by certain vaccines. The U.S. Court of Federal Claims decides who will be paid. Three Federal government offices have a role in the VICP:

- the U.S. Department of Health and Human Services (HHS);
- the U.S. Department of Justice (DOJ); and
- the U.S. Court of Federal Claims (the Court).

The VICP is located in the HHS, Health Resources and Services Administration, Healthcare Systems Bureau, Division of Vaccine Injury Compensation.

Chapter 3 – This is an edited, reformatted and augmented version of a report issued by the U.S. Department of Health and Human Services, February 2, 2015.

In: National Vaccine Injury Compensation ... ISBN: 978-1-63482-528-3
Editor: Preston Torres

Chapter 1

VACCINE INJURY COMPENSATION: MOST CLAIMS TOOK MULTIPLE YEARS AND MANY WERE SETTLED THROUGH NEGOTIATION*

United States Government Accountability Office

WHY GAO DID THIS STUDY

Vaccines save lives by preventing disease in the people who receive them. In some instances, however, a vaccine can have severe side effects, including death or an injury requiring lifetime medical care. VICP provides compensation to people for injuries and deaths associated with certain vaccines for medical and other costs. The program includes an injury table that lists the injuries that are presumed to be caused by vaccines covered by the program. The program may also compensate individuals for injuries not on the table; however, in those cases causation is not presumed. In both cases, medical and other records are required. VICP pays claims from a trust fund. Since the program began in 1988, it has awarded more than $2.8 billion in compensation.

* This is an edited, reformatted and augmented version of a United States Government Accountability Office publication, No. GAO-15-142, dated November 2014.

GAO was asked to review the program. GAO examined (1) how long it has taken to adjudicate claims and how claims have been adjudicated, (2) the changes to the vaccine injury table, and (3) how the balance of and spending from the Vaccine Injury Compensation Trust Fund have changed, among other objectives.

GAO examined data and interviewed officials from HHS, DOJ, and USCFC, including data on claims filed since fiscal year 1999 and their status as of March 31, 2014; reviewed laws and agency documents; and reviewed Treasury data and agency data on compensation and obligations for other VICP-related expenses for fiscal years 2009 through 2013.

HHS and USCFC agreed with GAO's findings, and HHS, USCFC, DOJ, and Treasury provided technical comments that were incorporated as appropriate.

WHAT GAO FOUND

Most of more than 9,800 claims filed with the National Vaccine Injury Compensation Program (VICP) since fiscal year 1999 have taken multiple years to adjudicate. More than 1,000 (11 percent) of claims filed since fiscal year 1999 were still in process (pending) as of March 31, 2014; most of these were pending for 2 years or less. A greater percentage of the claims filed since fiscal year 2009 were resolved within 1 or 2 years. In all but 1 year since fiscal year 2009, the program has met the target for the average time to adjudicate claims (about 3.5 years) tracked by the Department of Health and Human Services (HHS), which administers the program. Officials from the U.S. Court of Federal Claims (USCFC), where VICP claims are adjudicated, report that delays may occur while petitioners gather evidence for their claims. Since 2006, about 80 percent of compensated claims have been resolved through a negotiated settlement.

Since fiscal year 1999, HHS has added six vaccines to the vaccine injury table, but it has not added covered injuries associated with these vaccines to the table. This means that while individuals may file VICP claims for these vaccines, each petitioner must demonstrate that the vaccine that was administered caused the alleged injury. HHS is considering adding covered injuries associated with these vaccines; but as of September 2014, it had not published any final rules to do so.

The balance of the Vaccine Injury Compensation Trust Fund, managed by the Department of the Treasury (Treasury) increased from $2.9 billion in fiscal year 2009 to nearly $3.3 billion at the end of fiscal year 2013 as the trust fund's income (from net revenues from vaccine excise taxes and interest on investments) outpaced its disbursements to HHS, USCFC, and the Department of Justice (DOJ), which represents HHS in VICP proceedings. VICP compensation, funded by the trust fund, increased from less than $126 million in each of fiscal years 1999 to 2009 to over $254 million in fiscal year 2013.

ABBREVIATIONS

DOJ	Department of Justice
FTE	full-time equivalent
HHS	Department of Health and Human Services
HRSA	Health Resources and Services Administration
Treasury	Department of the Treasury
USCFC	U.S. Court of Federal Claims
VICP	National Vaccine Injury Compensation Program

* * *

November 21, 2014

The Honorable Darrell E. Issa
Chairman
Committee on Oversight and Government Reform
House of Representatives

Dear Mr. Chairman:

Vaccines save lives by preventing disease in the people who receive them. In some instances, however, a vaccine can have severe side effects, including death or an injury requiring lifetime medical care.[1] In the 1980s, lawsuits stemming from such incidents threatened to affect the availability and cost of vaccines as well as the development of new ones.

To address this issue, Congress established the National Vaccine Injury Compensation Program (VICP), which is administered by the Department of Health and Human Services (HHS).[2] People who believe they or their child have been injured by vaccines covered by the program may file a petition making a claim with VICP for compensation for medical and other costs and for pain and suffering, as an alternative to civil court.[3] The program uses a vaccine injury table that lists the injuries and conditions that are presumed to be caused by vaccines covered by the program and thus may entitle a petitioner to compensation. The program may also compensate petitioners for injuries or conditions that are not on the vaccine injury table; however, in those cases causation is not presumed and the petitioner must demonstrate that the vaccine caused the injury or condition. The program pays claims from the Vaccine Injury Compensation Trust Fund, a trust fund supported by an excise tax on each dose of a vaccine covered by the program; since the program began in 1988, more than 15,000 claims had been filed and more than $2.8 billion has been awarded to petitioners.

In 1999, we reported that while the program appears to provide an easier process for obtaining compensation than through the civil court system, the claims process was not as quick or easy as expected.[4] Recently, concerns have been raised about the timeliness for adjudicating VICP claims and making changes to the vaccine injury table, how the funds in the Vaccine Injury Compensation Trust Fund have been spent, and petitioner experiences and awareness of the program. You asked that we examine these issues. Specifically, this report examines (1) how long it has taken to adjudicate VICP claims and how claims have been adjudicated, (2) the changes to the vaccine injury table and in the types of claims filed, (3) how the balance of and spending from the trust fund have changed, and (4) available information on petitioner experience with VICP and how HHS has informed the public of the availability of VICP.

To address these questions, we used data and information from the federal agencies involved in administering the program and managing the Vaccine Injury Compensation Trust Fund, and from stakeholders. Specifically, to examine how long it has taken to adjudicate VICP claims we examined VICP data and interviewed officials from HHS's Health Resources and Services Administration (HRSA), which administers VICP; the Department of Justice (DOJ), which represents HHS in VICP proceedings; and the U.S. Court of Federal Claims (USCFC) and the Office of Special Masters within USCFC that adjudicates, or decides, VICP claims.[5] We analyzed USCFC data to examine time frames for the adjudication of claims filed in fiscal years 1999-2014.[6] To examine changes to the vaccine injury table and in the types of claims filed, we reviewed relevant laws, and other documents, including Federal Register notices, studies conducted for HHS by the Institute of Medicine, and HRSA's proposals for revising the vaccine injury table since fiscal year 1999, and interviewed officials from HRSA and members of its

Advisory Commission on Childhood Vaccines.[7] We also examined HRSA data on the numbers of claims filed, by vaccine, and USCFC data on the number of claims alleging injuries on the vaccine injury table. To examine the balance of and spending from the Vaccine Injury Compensation Trust Fund, we reviewed reports from the Department of the Treasury (Treasury), which manages the trust fund, to determine the income into and disbursements from the trust fund for fiscal years 2009-2013. We also analyzed HRSA data on the amounts the agency reported for petitioner compensation and attorneys' fees and costs, and data from HRSA, DOJ, and USCFC on the amounts they obligated for administrative and other expenses related to processing VICP claims for those fiscal years using appropriations from the trust fund.[8] Finally, to examine available information on petitioner experience with VICP and how HHS has informed the public of the availability of VICP, we reviewed documents, including the Public Health Service Act, agencies' congressional budget justifications, agency strategic plans, and studies prepared for HHS. We also reviewed statements and interviewed officials from HRSA, DOJ, and USCFC and stakeholders (from organizations representing providers, petitioners' attorneys, and parents) regarding available information on petitioner experiences with VICP and steps HHS has taken to inform the public about the availability of the program.[9] We determined that the data we used from HRSA, DOJ, and USCFC and from Treasury reports on the trust fund were sufficiently reliable for our purposes by discussing data collection processes and limitations of the data with agency officials, conducting electronic data checks, and comparing the data against other published sources.

We conducted this performance audit from February 2014 to November 2014 in accordance with generally accepted government auditing standards. Those standards require that we plan and perform the audit to obtain sufficient, appropriate evidence to provide a reasonable basis for our findings and conclusions based on our audit objectives. We believe that the evidence obtained provides a reasonable basis for our findings and conclusions based on our audit objectives.

BACKGROUND

In general, individuals seeking compensation for a vaccine-related injury or death must first file a petition making a claim for compensation under VICP before suing in civil court.[10] Several federal agencies—HHS, DOJ, and

USCFC, are involved in administering VICP, and Treasury manages the trust fund which funds compensation for successful claims.

Vaccines Covered by the Program and on the Vaccine Injury Table

VICP includes a vaccine injury table that lists the vaccines covered by the program and the injuries associated with each those vaccines. (See app. I for the table.) Vaccines are added to the list covered by the program after the Centers for Disease Control and Prevention recommends them for routine administration to children and they are made subject to an excise tax that funds the Vaccine Injury Compensation Trust Fund.[11] When individuals submit a claim for an injury listed on the table (called an on-table injury), they do not need to prove that the injury was caused by the vaccine. Instead, if they submit documentation showing that they received a particular vaccine and that they sustained the associated covered injury within the time interval specified on the table, they may receive compensation based on a presumption of causation (unless there is evidence that the injury is due to other factors).[12] Individuals seeking compensation may submit claims for injuries not listed on the table (called off-table injuries) but they need to demonstrate by the preponderance of the evidence that the vaccine caused the alleged injury.[13]

HHS has authority to promulgate rules to modify the vaccine injury table when certain criteria are met. [14] HHS is also required to amend the table to include a vaccine within 2 years of the Centers for Disease Control and Prevention's recommending it for routine administration to children.[15] The Advisory Commission on Childhood Vaccines, which was established by the act creating the program, is required to make recommendations concerning changes to the table.[16] In 1999, GAO reported that HHS added seven injuries and removed three others from the table in 1995 and 1997, respectively, using findings from Institute of Medicine reviews conducted in 1991 and 1994—in conjunction with public policy considerations provided by the Advisory Commission on Childhood Vaccines, scientific issues raised by HHS's National Vaccine Advisory Committee, and input from the public.[17]

VICP Claims Process

Individuals who believe they or their child have been injured by or a death resulted from a vaccine covered by the program may file a petition making a claim with the USCFC.[18] In general, to be eligible for compensation, a petition must be filed (1) for a vaccine-related injury within 3 years of the first symptom of the injury (or significant aggravation of an injury), or (2) for a death within 2 years of the death and within 4 years after the first symptom of the vaccine-related injury (or signification aggravation of an injury) from which the death resulted.[19]

HHS, as the respondent in the process, receives a copy of the petition, including medical records, and other documentation filed with the USCFC. HRSA sends a report of its medical review including HHS's recommendation regarding the claim to DOJ. DOJ lawyers, representing HHS in the proceedings, review the HRSA report and the legal aspects of the claim and produce a report that outlines the government's position as to why compensation should or should not be awarded, provides a summary and medical analysis of the petitioner's claims, and asserts applicable legal arguments.

After the claim is filed in USCFC, it is assigned to a special master, a judicial officer who examines the evidence and adjudicates the claim.[20] The special master reviews the petition and may order the petitioner to provide additional records if they are missing or if they are insufficient.[21] Additionally, petitioners and DOJ may file expert reports including additional medical evidence from scientific literature or studies. The special master then determines whether a claim should be compensated.[22]

For claims that are compensated, there are three adjudication categories:

- **Concession**. In a concession, HHS's review of medical records, scientific literature, and other documents finds that the petitioner is entitled to compensation, because the evidence meets the criteria of the vaccine injury table or because it is more likely than not that the vaccine caused the injury.
- **Negotiated settlement**. In a negotiated settlement, the petition is resolved via negotiation between HHS (represented by DOJ) and the petitioner.[23]
- **Contested decision in favor of the petitioner**. If HHS does not concede that a petition should be compensated or if both parties do not agree to settle, the special master issues a decision after weighing

the evidence presented by both sides, which may involve conducting a hearing.[24]

If the petitioner is entitled to compensation as a result of a concession or contested decision in favor of the petitioner, the proceeding then moves to the damages phase, in which the amount of compensation is determined.[25] In a negotiated settlement, the amount of compensation is included in the settlement presented to the special master. VICP may also pay for attorneys' fees and costs deemed reasonable even for unsuccessful petitioners, and the amounts of these fees and costs may be part of a settlement between the parties or determined by the special masters.[26] After the claim has been adjudicated within VICP, the petitioner may choose to file a suit in civil court. Even if found to be entitled to compensation, the petitioner may elect to reject the compensation awarded and file a suit in civil court.[27]

The Vaccine Injury Compensation Trust Fund, managed by Treasury, is funded by an excise tax imposed on each dose of vaccine sold in the United States that is routinely recommended for administration to children.[28] Appropriations from the trust fund to HRSA pay compensation awarded under VICP for vaccine-related injury or death to the petitioner and may also pay for petitioner attorneys' fees and costs. Appropriations from the trust fund to HRSA, DOJ, and USCFC (for the Office of Special Masters) also pay for administrative and other expenses associated with processing VICP claims.[29]

USCFC has managed large influxes of similar vaccine injury claims through omnibus proceedings or groupings of claims. According to the Office of Special Masters, many of the claims alleging that a particular vaccine caused the same injury will rely on similar evidence, so by using omnibus proceedings or groupings to examine evidence for similar claims, the courts can more efficiently review the evidence.[30] In omnibus proceedings, petitioners select a lead claim in each category of injury, and develop these lead claims while the remaining petitioners choosing to participate in the omnibus elect for their remaining claims to be stayed, or put on hold, until the lead claim reaches a final disposition.

Requirements for Disseminating Information on the Program

HHS is required to include a statement of the availability of VICP in the vaccine information materials that health care providers are to distribute to the parent or legal representatives of a child or to any other individual to whom the provider intends to administer a covered vaccine.[31] These materials—referred to as vaccine information statements by HHS—are intended to explain both the benefits and risks of a vaccine covered by VICP. HHS is also required to undertake reasonable efforts to inform the public of the availability of the program.[32]

Most Claims Took Multiple Years to Adjudicate and Many Were Adjudicated by Settlement or Addressed by an Omnibus Proceeding

Most of the VICP claims filed since fiscal year 1999 have taken multiple years to adjudicate, but those filed since fiscal year 2009 have taken less time. For many claims, the parties have concluded the proceeding through a negotiated settlement, rather than a contested decision adjudicated by a special master or the courts. Additionally, certain claims were addressed along with similar claims as part of an omnibus proceeding or informal grouping.

Most Claims Filed Since Fiscal Year 1999 Have Taken Multiple Years to Adjudicate

VICP claims filed since fiscal year 1999 took an average of about 5 and a half years to adjudicate, according to USCFC data for the nearly 8,800 claims filed since fiscal year 1999 that were adjudicated as of March 31, 2014.[33] There was wide variation in the amount of time to adjudicate these claims. The claim that took the shortest time to adjudicate was filed in fiscal year 1999 and took 2 days, and the claim that took the longest time to adjudicate was filed in fiscal year 1999 and took 5,276 days (more than 14 years). More than 1,000 (11 percent) of the claims filed since fiscal year 1999 were still in process (pending) as of March 31, 2014; most of these had been pending for 2 years or less (see fig. 1.)

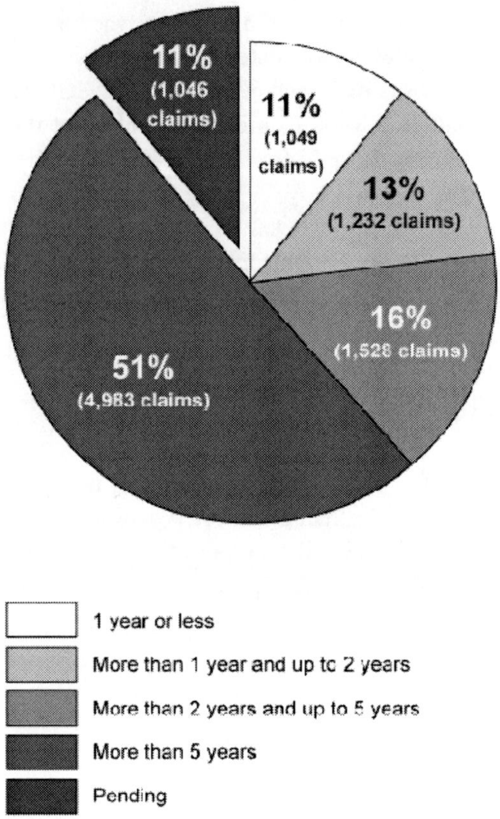

Source: GAO analysis of U.S. Court of Federal Claims data. | GAO-15-142.

Note: This figure shows the time (as of March 31, 2014) to adjudicate claims for which petitions were filed in fiscal year 1999 through March 31, 2014, based on data from the U.S. Court of Federal Claims. Figures do not sum to 100 due to rounding.

Figure 1. Time Taken to Adjudicate National Vaccine Injury Compensation Program Claims Filed Fiscal Years 1999-2014, as of March 31, 2014.

For claims filed since fiscal year 2009, a greater percentage of claims were resolved within 1 or 2 years. One possible reason is that the vast majority of claims alleging autism as the injury were filed prior to fiscal year 2009. Autism claims may have taken longer because they were part of an omnibus proceeding, which suspended activity on most autism claims for a period of time. According to USCFC data, for the more than 1,400 claims filed since fiscal year 2009 that were adjudicated as of March 31, 2014, the average amount of time to adjudicate a claim was 587 days (about 1.6 years). More than 900 (40 percent) of the claims filed since fiscal year 1999 were still pending, which could cause this average to increase over time as these pending claims are resolved (see fig. 2).[34] Of the pending claims, nearly half had been pending for 1 year or less as of March 31, 2014.

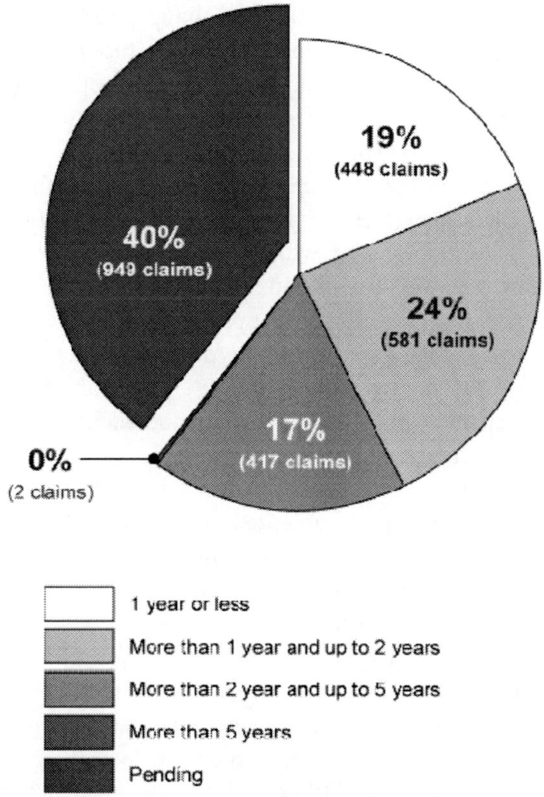

Source: GAO analysis of U.S. Court of Federal Claims data. I GAO-15-142.

Note: This figure shows the status (as of March 31, 2014) of nearly 2,400 claims for which petitions were filed in fiscal year 2009 through March 31, 2014, based on data from the U.S. Court of Federal Claims.

Figure 2. Status of National Vaccine Injury Compensation Program Claims Filed Fiscal Years 2009-2014, as of March 31, 2014.

HHS has reported the program has met its annual target of 1,300 days (about 3.5 years) for the average time to adjudicate non-autism claims in all but 1 year since fiscal year 2009. This target (1,300 days) has been in place since fiscal year 2009, and applies to claims concluded in a given fiscal year, regardless of the year they were filed, excluding claims that alleged autism as the vaccine-related injury.[35] HRSA has reported meeting this goal since fiscal year 2009, except in fiscal year 2012, when VICP claims concluded that year took an average of 1,309 days to complete.

Organizations representing petitioners have criticized the program for taking a long time to resolve claims. Petitioners report that long processing times delay receiving compensation to pay medical bills and other expenses related to the alleged injury. A HRSA-contracted survey of petitioners whose claims were adjudicated (regardless of whether or not they received compensation under VICP), found that nearly two-thirds of the 103 respondents indicated they were somewhat or very dissatisfied with the length of the process. [36] Petitioners may withdraw if a VICP decision is not made on their claim within specific time periods but according to the Office of Special Masters, petitioners rarely exercise this option.[37]

Officials cite certain delays within the process as factors that can increase average claims processing times. Officials at USCFC and DOJ told us that the time petitioners spend gathering supporting documentation or evidence can add significantly to the amount of time required to process a claim. These delays may occur at multiple points in the claims process, from petitioners needing to gather sufficient documentation for the court to begin an initial review, to the court needing documentation to determine the amount of compensation that a successful petitioner will receive.[38] According to HRSA, for claims adjudicated as of March 31, 2014, its medical review process averaged over 700 days for claims filed in fiscal year 2010. HRSA attributes the length of time for medical review primarily to time spent waiting for petitioners to submit requested documentation. During the medical review, HRSA may also consult with external experts, who require additional time to review the details of the case; HRSA's data indicate that over 1,200 outside reviews were conducted from fiscal years 2009 to 2014. Additionally, when special masters are reviewing the claim, a party may request that the special master delay a decision until additional documentation is available.[39] Special masters may also request additional information from petitioners—such as a specialist physician's opinion.

Many Claims Were Adjudicated through Settlement or Grouped in an Omnibus Autism Proceeding

According to HRSA data for claims filed since 2006, most compensated claims were adjudicated through negotiated settlement rather than a concession or a contested decision. HRSA's data indicated that about 80 percent of the more than 1,500 non-autism VICP claims filed since 2006 for which compensation was awarded were adjudicated through a negotiated settlement between the parties, compared to about 10 percent involving a contested decision in favor of the petitioner and about 10 percent conceded by HHS.[40] According to HRSA, claims which HHS does not concede may be resolved via a negotiated settlement for several reasons, including a desire by both parties to resolve a case quickly and efficiently. According to the Office of Special Masters, a special master may recommend parties settle as an expeditious and efficient method of resolving certain claims.

The Office of Special Masters created an omnibus proceeding in order to address thousands of autism cases systematically and efficiently.[41] Beginning in 1999, parents began filing petitions for compensation under VICP alleging that autism or neurodevelopmental disorders similar to autism were caused by the measles-mumps-rubella vaccine or vaccines containing thimerosal, a mercury-containing preservative used in some vaccines, covered by the program, or both.

In 2002, the Office of Special Masters held a series of meetings with an informal advisory committee, including attorneys who represented many potential petitioners and legal and medical representatives of HHS, to address the task of dealing with these claims. The Office of Special Masters decided to utilize a two-step procedure: first, looking into whether the vaccinations in question can cause autism and, if so, the circumstances under which this occurs, and second, applying the conclusions from the first step to the individual claims.

The omnibus autism proceeding included test cases for two different theories by which vaccines were alleged to cause autism.[42] Some petitioners withdrew from the omnibus proceeding and elected to proceed within the vaccine program on other theories of causation. Some petitioners withdrew from the program entirely, as was their statutory right, which enabled them to pursue claims against vaccine manufacturers in civil court.[43]

The influx of new VICP claims for autism continued in fiscal years 2002-2005, while the number of new non-autism claims remained relatively stable (see fig. 3).

HRSA data show that during this period, nearly 90 percent of VICP claims filed alleged autism as the vaccine-related injury. Ultimately, the special masters did not award compensation in any of the test cases,[44] and most remaining omnibus autism proceeding claims were dismissed. However, according to the Office of Special Masters, some petitioners who had been part of the omnibus autism proceeding continued with claims separate from the omnibus proceeding.[45]

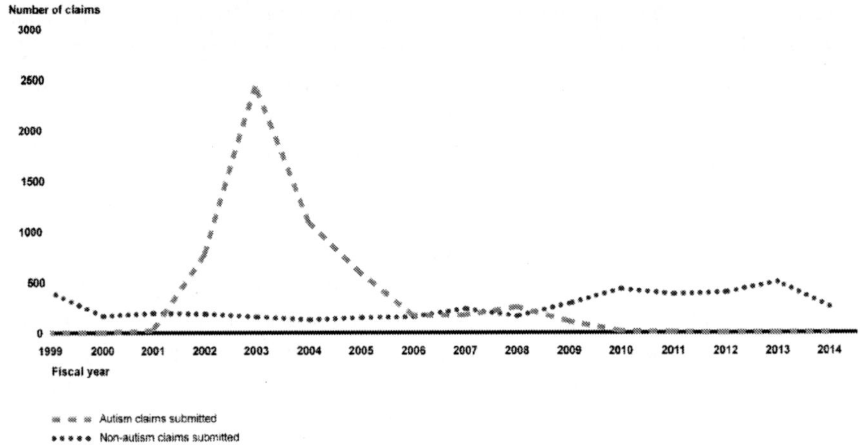

Source: GAO analysis of Health Resources and Services Administration data. | GAO-15-142.

Note: Data for fiscal year 2014 are as of March 31, 2014.

Figure 3. Number of National Vaccine Injury Compensation Program Claims Filed Alleging Autism, Fiscal Years 1999-2014, as of March 31, 2014.

VACCINES HAVE BEEN ADDED TO THE VACCINE INJURY TABLE SINCE FISCAL YEAR 1999 WITHOUT COVERED INJURIES, RESULTING IN MORE OFF-TABLE CLAIMS

HHS has added vaccines to the vaccine injury table without adding covered injuries associated with those vaccines. Following their addition to the table, more claims were filed for off-table injuries.

Six Vaccines Have Been Added to the Vaccine Injury Table since Fiscal Year 1999 without Covered Injuries; HHS Is Considering Additional Changes

Since fiscal year 1999, HHS has added six vaccines to the vaccine injury table (but has not added covered injuries associated with these vaccines to the table).[46] This means that while individuals may file VICP claims for those vaccines, each petitioner must demonstrate that the vaccine that was administered caused the alleged injury. In general, each of the six vaccines was added within 2 years of the Centers for Disease Control and Prevention's recommending it for routine administration to children and having an excise tax imposed.[47] Since 1999, two vaccines, both of which had covered injuries associated with them, were removed from the vaccine injury table.[48] See appendix II for the vaccines and injuries added and removed from the vaccine injury table since 1999. At the end of the fiscal year 2014, 16 vaccines were covered by the program, 8 of which did not have associated covered injuries on the table.[49]

HHS has been considering adding injuries to the table in association with the eight vaccines that are listed without covered injuries.[50] Specifically, HRSA officials said they are working on a final rule to add an injury associated with one vaccine and a proposed rule that would add injuries associated with several other vaccines.

- In July 2013, HRSA published a proposed rule to add intussusception (obstruction of the bowels) as an injury associated with the rotavirus vaccine.[51] In proposing the addition, HRSA considered reviews and injury claims attributed to another vaccine that protected against rotavirus but had been removed from the table in fiscal year 2009. According to HRSA, the agency is working on a final rule to add this injury.
- HRSA officials said they are developing a proposed rule to add covered injuries for all seven of the remaining vaccines on the table without covered injuries. For example, HRSA is considering proposing to add Guillain-Barré Syndrome (a disorder in which the body's immune system attacks part of the nervous system and is characterized by muscle weakness and paralysis), as an injury associated with the influenza vaccine. The agency is also considering proposing to add other injuries associated with the influenza, hemophilus influenza type b conjugate, varicella, pneumococcal

conjugate, hepatitis A, meningococcal, and human papillomavirus vaccines.

According to HRSA officials, the factors informing the table changes that they are considering proposing include (1) an Institute of Medicine study of certain vaccines;[52] (2) HHS's independent review of vaccine causation and medical and scientific evidence; (3) the need to clarify injury definitions on the table[53] ; and (4) recent studies related to injuries associated with the influenza vaccine.

As of September 30, 2014, HRSA had not promulgated regulations to make these changes to the vaccine injury table. According to HRSA officials, the agency plans

- to publish the final rule to add the injury associated with the rotavirus vaccine to the table by July 2015,[54] and
- to publish a proposed rule for the other injuries it is considering adding to the table by August 2015.

According to HRSA officials, the process to publish such a proposed rule can take about 9 months to 1.5 years. The officials also said that the process for publishing such a final rule can take about 1.5 years to 2.5 years after the proposed rule is published.

In its justification accompanying its fiscal year 2013 budget request, HRSA acknowledged that many stakeholders, including Congress, have voiced interest and concern over keeping the injury table in line with current science. At that time, HRSA reported that other VICP activities, including medical reviews and court deadlines, have taken priority over updating the table.[55]

While the injuries HRSA is considering have not yet been added to the table, HRSA and DOJ officials report that many claims alleging these injuries that HRSA is considering adding to the table have been conceded or settled. For example, according to DOJ officials, there have been numerous settlements for cases alleging Guillain-Barré Syndrome as an injury associated with the influenza vaccine.

Changes in the Vaccine Injury Table Contributed to More Claims for Off-Table Injuries and for Injuries in Adults

The addition of the six vaccines to the vaccine injury table without associated injuries has contributed to an increase in off-table claims. When we reported on this program in 1999, 2 of the 12 vaccines on the injury table were without associated injuries listed on the table. We reported that about one-quarter (28 percent) of claims filed as of February 1999 were for off-table injuries.[56] In contrast, of the 3,007 claims filed since fiscal year 2005 (the year that trivalent influenza vaccine was added to the table) for which the covered vaccine associated with the alleged injury was specified, at least 59 percent were associated with one of five vaccines added to the table without associated table injuries, according to HRSA data.[57] To receive compensation, the petitioners in these claims would not have the presumption of causation associated with an on-table claim. Overall, since 2009, more than 98 percent of the new claims filed alleged off-table injuries that required the petitioner to prove their injury was caused by the vaccine they received, according to the Office of Special Masters. Claims alleging injuries to adults also increased as a result of the addition of vaccines that are recommended for administration in adults (as well as children) to the vaccine injury table. Several of the vaccines added to the injury table—in particular, the vaccine to prevent influenza—are recommended for routine administration to adults as well as children.[58] As a result, although the vaccines were added to the table because they were recommended for children, adults who are vaccinated with them are also eligible for compensation under VICP. More than half (51 percent) of the 4,402 VICP claims filed since fiscal year 1999 (for which the covered vaccine associated with the alleged injury was specified) were for injuries to adults and 1,287 (29 percent) were for adults alleging injuries in association with influenza vaccine, according to HRSA data.[59]

TRUST FUND BALANCE HAS INCREASED SINCE 2009, AS HAS PETITIONER AND ATTORNEY COMPENSATION AND OTHER VICP-RELATED SPENDING

The Vaccine Injury Compensation Trust Fund balance increased to more than $3 billion in fiscal year 2013 despite increased spending by HRSA, DOJ, and USCFC on petitioner compensation, attorneys' fees and costs, and other VICP-related expenses.

From Fiscal Year 2009 to 2013 the Trust Fund Balance Gradually Increased to More than $3 Billion

The balance in the trust fund increased from $2.9 billion at the end of fiscal year 2009 to nearly $3.3 billion at the end of fiscal year 2013.[60] The balance increased because the trust fund's income outpaced its disbursements to HRSA, DOJ, and USCFC, although disbursements also increased during this period (see fig. 4).[61]

Treasury reported over $200 million in net revenues from the vaccine excise tax in each of fiscal years 2009-2013. As required by applicable law pertaining to the management of trust funds, Treasury oversees the investment of part of the net revenue from vaccine excise taxes.[62] Interest from these investments ranged from about $49 million in fiscal year 2012 to about $126 million in fiscal year 2011.

Spending on Compensation to Petitioners and Attorneys Has Increased since Fiscal Year 1999

Total compensation to petitioners and the number of claims compensated have both increased since fiscal year 1999. Petitioners' compensation paid by HRSA using appropriations from the trust fund increased to over $254 million in fiscal year 2013. With the exception of fiscal year 2000, the total amount spent on compensation awarded to petitioners remained under $125 million between fiscal years 1999 and 2009. The total amount spent on compensation to petitioners increased to nearly $180 million in fiscal year 2010 and to more than $250 million in fiscal year 2013 (see fig. 5 and app. III).[63]

According to the Office of Special Masters, the increase in the total amount paid to petitioners in compensation and number of compensated claims is related to the addition of the influenza vaccine to the vaccine injury table. The influenza vaccine, which is administered to millions of people each year, was added to the injury table in fiscal year 2005.

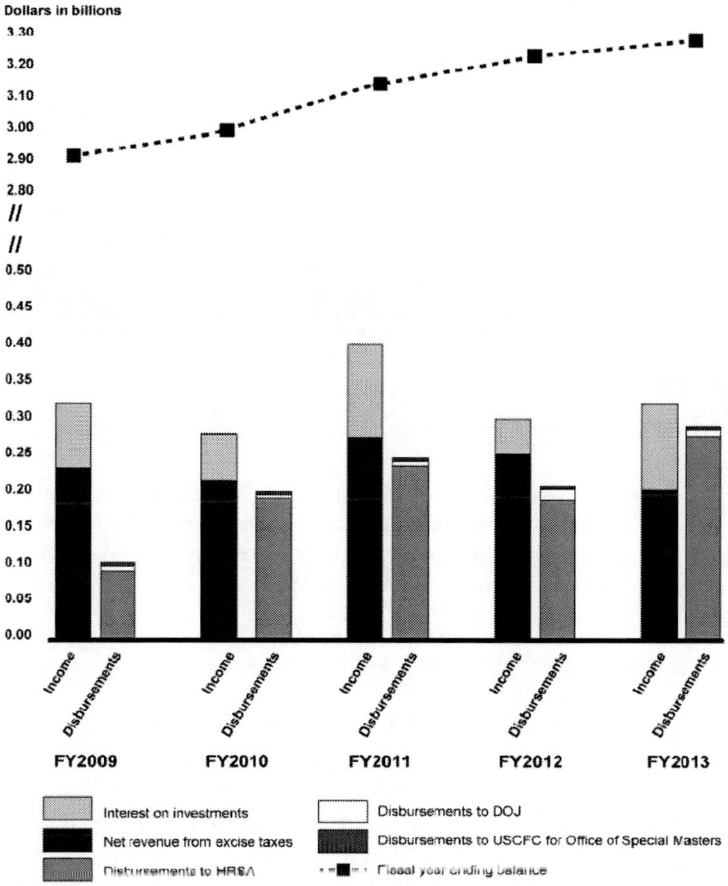

Source: GAO analysis of Treasury data. | GAO-15-142.

Note: This figure presents the Vaccine Injury Compensation Trust Fund balance (in terms of investment in U.S. securities issued by the Bureau of Fiscal Service and the fund balance with Treasury) at the end of the fiscal year. It also presents the income to trust fund (in terms of net revenue from excise taxes on vaccines and interest on investments) as well as disbursements to the Health Resources and Services Administration (HRSA)—for compensation to petitioners, attorneys' fees and costs, and administrative expenses, and to the Department of Justice (DOJ) and the U.S. Court of Federal Claims (USCFC) for the Office of Special Masters—for expenses associated with processing National Vaccine Injury Compensation Program (VICP) claims, as reported in the Treasury reports.

Figure 4. Vaccine Injury Compensation Trust Fund Income, Disbursements, and Balance for Fiscal Years 2009–2013.

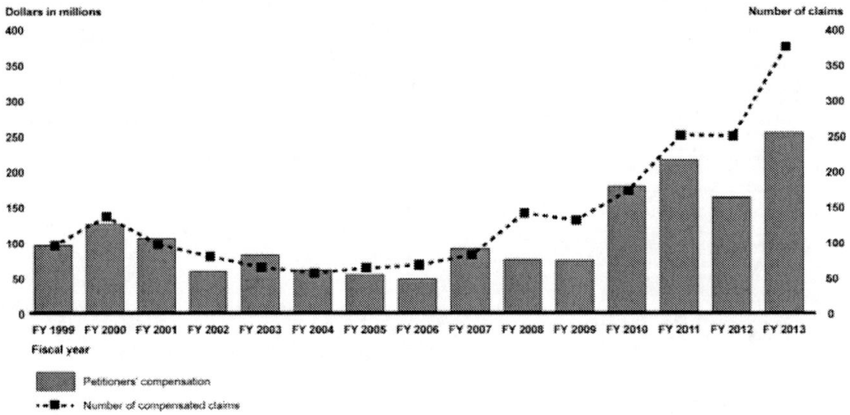

Source: GAO analysis of Health Resources and Services Administration data. | GAO-15-142.

Note: This figure presents the total amounts and numbers of claims paid by the Health Resources and Services Administration to petitioners under the National Vaccine Injury Compensation Program for each of fiscal years 1999-2013. Data are presented by the fiscal year in which the compensation was paid.

Figure 5. Compensation to Petitioners under the National Vaccine Injury Compensation Program.

The annual amount the VICP program paid for attorneys' fees and costs remained relatively steady from fiscal year 1999 to fiscal year 2007, but started to increase in fiscal year 2008, consistent with an increase in the total number of payments to attorneys (see fig. 6 and app. III). In order to help ensure access to the program, VICP may pay for reasonable attorney fees and costs upon a determination that the petition was brought in good faith and there was a reasonable basis for the claim for which the petition was brought, regardless of whether the petitioner's claim is compensated or dismissed.[64] The majority of VICP payments for attorneys' fees and costs have been for compensated or dismissed claims; however, since fiscal year 2008, VICP has also paid some interim attorneys' fees and costs for selected ongoing claims at the special master's discretion.[65] Compensation for attorneys' fees and costs must be reasonable such that it generally reflects the actual time and expense devoted to the case.

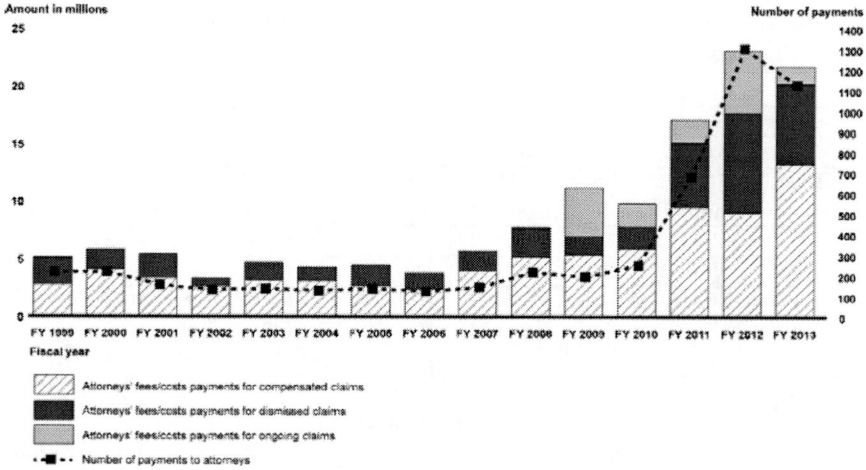

Source: GAO analysis of Health Resources and Services Administration data. | GAO-15-142.

Note: This figure presents the total amounts paid in attorneys' fees and costs for each fiscal year (based on the fiscal year in which the payment was made). Attorneys' fees and costs reflect the actual time and expense devoted to the case as opposed to a percentage of the compensation.

Figure 6. Payments to Attorneys under the National Vaccine Injury Compensation Program.

Spending on Agency Staff and Other VICP-Related Expenses Has Increased

The total amount obligated by HRSA, DOJ, and USCFC (for the Office of Special Masters) to pay for staff and other expenses related to processing VICP claims increased from $17 million in fiscal year 2009 to about $19 million in fiscal year 2013.[66] The three departments obligated a total of about $91 million for expenses associated with processing VICP claims during those 5 fiscal years. About two-thirds of VICP-related expenses ($61 million) was obligated to pay the salaries and benefits of full-time equivalent (FTE) agency staff and about one-third ($30 million) was obligated for other VICP-related expenses (see table 1).

Table 1. Amounts Obligated by HRSA, DOJ, and USCFC for the National Vaccine Injury Compensation Program Administrative Expenses

Dollars in millions							
	HRSA[a]		**DOJ**		**USCFC**[b]		
Fiscal year	**FTE staff (number)**	**Other expenses**	**FTE staff (number)**	**Other expenses**	**FTE staff (number)**	**Other expenses**	**Total obligations**
2009	$2.8 (18)	$2.6	$4.5 (34)	$3.2	$3.2 (24)	$0.8	**$17.0**
2010	3.4 (22)	3.1	5.0 (34)	2.5	3.3 (25)	1.7	**19.0**
2011	3.8 (22)	2.7	5.4 (33)	2.4	3.4 (26)	0.8	**18.5**
2012	4.2 (22)	2.3	5.4 (34)	1.6	3.7 (29)	1.0	**18.1**
2013	3.8 (20)	2.5	5.5 (34)	2.1	3.7 (29)	1.1	**18.7**
Total	**$17.9**	**$13.2**	**$25.8**	**$11.9**	**$17.3**	**$5.4**	**$91.4**

Source: GAO summary of HHS, DOJ, and USCFC data. | GAO-15-142

Legend: HRSA = Health Resources and Services Administration; DOJ = Department of Justice; USCFC = U.S. Court of Federal Claims; FTE = Full-time equivalent.

Notes: Figures do not sum to totals due to rounding.

[a]Amounts obligated by HRSA do not include compensation to petitioners or attorney costs. [b]Amounts obligated by USCFC were for the Office of Special Masters.

The amounts obligated for FTE salaries and benefits were for staff of HRSA, DOJ, and USCFC's Office of Special Masters who process the claims and represent the government's interest in legal proceedings. For example, USCFC's Office of Special Masters paid the salaries and benefits for special masters and clerks. The average number of full-time equivalent (FTE) staff supported across the three agencies was 81 per fiscal year.

Each agency also had other VICP-related spending reimbursed by the trust fund. For example, HRSA reported obligating about $9.6 million for medical experts to review petitioner claims and provide expert testimony during adjudication proceedings for fiscal years 2009 through 2013. HRSA also obligated funds to support the Advisory Commission on Childhood Vaccines, including compensation and travel expenses for commission members. The departments reported obligating funds for costs for travel, processing documents, maintaining records, rent, supplies, and equipment. For example, obligations include rental payments to the General Services Administration by DOJ and the cost of court reporters funded by USCFC's Office of Special Masters.

INFORMATION ON VICP PETITIONER EXPERIENCE IS LIMITED; HHS IS TAKING STEPS TO ADDRESS CRITICISM OF ITS OUTREACH EFFORTS

Information on petitioners' experience with VICP is limited. HRSA has taken some steps to undertake outreach activities, but the agency has not yet assessed the effect of these efforts.

Information on Petitioners' Experiences with VICP Is Limited

Other than a study for HRSA on petitioners' satisfaction with VICP, the agency officials and stakeholders we interviewed and the documents we reviewed did not identify any data or studies regarding the experience of individuals who have filed VICP claims. The study prepared for HRSA, dated 2009, reported the responses from 107 petitioners whose claims were compensated or dismissed in fiscal years 2004-2008. Because this was a voluntary survey with a low response rate, its results cannot be generalized to all petitioners who completed the VICP process; instead, it reflects only the experience of the VICP petitioners who responded to the survey.[67] We also obtained comments from stakeholders, including officials from organizations representing providers, petitioners' attorneys, and parents. These stakeholder comments, while providing insight into petitioner experiences, are anecdotal and do not represent the experience of all petitioners who have filed VICP claims. Members of the Advisory Commission on Childhood Vaccines we interviewed expressed interest in obtaining additional information on petitioner's experience with VICP; however, they told us they had not done so, citing concerns about confidentiality and other issues.

The limited comments on petitioners' experience from those who responded to the survey prepared for HRSA and from stakeholders included the following:

- Some petitioners responding to the HRSA survey reported being dissatisfied with the claims process and some commented that the process places too great a burden on petitioners and family members, with requests for additional information after the claims were filed. Similarly, one stakeholder said that petitioners view the vaccine injury claims process as confusing, time-consuming, too lengthy, and traumatic. Another stakeholder, on the other hand, commented that while vaccine-related injuries do not happen often, the program handles them efficiently and fairly when they do happen.

- Other comments from petitioners responding to the HRSA survey and stakeholders were related to the payment process and amount of compensation. More than half of the 61 petitioners who responded to a question on the method of payment in the HRSA survey reported being somewhat or very satisfied with the method of award payment; however, 14 respondents suggested more timely and flexible payment mechanisms. About half of the 63 respondents to the question on the amount of compensation reported the award amount was inadequate to cover past and future medical care. Similarly, stakeholders we interviewed reported concerns with the amounts petitioners receive, the method of payment, and a perceived lack of transparency regarding how the money from the Vaccine Injury Compensation Trust Fund has been spent. For example, one stakeholder told us that petitioners felt forced to settle for less than what it will cost them to care for their children or themselves for their lifetimes, and another stakeholder raised concerns about the choice of annuities for petitioners.
- Other comments on the program from stakeholders were related to the perception of an adversarial or unfriendly environment throughout the process, the use of settlements and perceived pressure to settle claims, the use of omnibus proceedings to group claims together, and concerns about confidentiality of the medical information filed by the petitioner. Some petitioners responding to the HRSA survey and some stakeholders also reported difficulties finding an attorney to represent petitioners in the process; however, petitioners responding to the survey were split on this issue—about the same number reported that finding an attorney was difficult as reported that finding an attorney was easy.

HHS Is Taking Steps to Address Criticism of Its Efforts to Inform the Public of the Program

HRSA has acknowledged being criticized for years for not adequately promoting public awareness of VICP, and has recently taken some steps, such as developing and starting to implement an outreach plan for fiscal year 2014 and developing an outreach plan for fiscal year 2015, to improve its efforts to reach out to providers and the public.[68] In its 2006 VICP strategic plan, HRSA noted that one of the critical issues facing the program from 2005 to 2010 was that many parents, the general public, attorneys, and health care professionals were not aware VICP existed.[69] In 2009, HRSA contracted for the development of a comprehensive national marketing and outreach communication plan; the contactor presented the plan to HRSA in November 2010.[70] According to HRSA, the agency used this plan to guide outreach efforts.[71] Prior to the fiscal year 2014 plan, HRSA also reported exhibiting at professional conferences; updating the VICP website and the VICP booklet that is available from the website (including translating the booklet into Spanish); facilitating the review of vaccine information statements (which include a statement on VICP) by the Advisory Commission on Childhood Vaccines; and responding to media inquiries and inquiries received via e-mail, letters, and the program's toll-free number.[72] HRSA officials also noted the need to carefully balance messages that increase awareness of VICP with public health messages that encourage and promote immunizations.

HRSA shared an overview of its outreach plans with its Advisory Commission on Childhood Vaccines in September 2014. HRSA reported that many of the activities in the agency's 2014 outreach plan were in process at the end of the fiscal year. These activities included reviewing the VICP booklets to use plain language and make them more user-friendly, reviewing and upgrading the VICP website to improve navigation, developing VICP message points for target audiences and slides about the program to be used in speeches and other presentations by HRSA staff, and requesting federal websites to provide information on the program and to link to the VICP website. In its outreach plan for fiscal year 2015, the agency is targeting health care providers, parents and expectant parents, adults aged 50 years and older (including Spanish-speaking older adults), and civil litigation and health attorneys, with the goal of informing target audiences of the availability of the program. According to HRSA, these target audiences were selected because they include individuals who administer vaccines and individuals (or their caregivers) who receive vaccinations. HRSA has identified a number of measures to assist in tracking performance of its fiscal year 2015 plan, including website metrics, the number of "retweets" and "shares" from social media initiatives, the number of media inquiries, and the number of attendees or participants at outreach events. Because the agency has not completed many of its planned efforts to improve how it informs the public of the availability of the program, it is too early to determine the effect of HRSA's current and planned outreach efforts.

Without awareness of the program, individuals who might otherwise receive compensation for a vaccine-related injury or death could be denied compensation because of a failure to file their claim within the statutory deadlines. One stakeholder commented that the public is largely unaware of the program, and this lack of awareness contributes to missing filing deadlines and individuals being denied the opportunity for compensation. Members of the Advisory Commission on Childhood Vaccines also told us that many individuals may not know there is a statute of limitations on filing a claim and many miss the opportunity to file a claim because of the statute of limitations.[73] In December 2013, the commission recommended extending the statute of limitations for vaccine-related injuries and deaths. Extending the statute of limitations would require amending the applicable statutory provision.[74]

CONCLUDING OBSERVATIONS

It has been more than 25 years since VICP went into effect in 1988. In that time, the program has awarded more than $2.8 billion to thousands of petitioners. Several aspects of the program have changed over the years. First, while claims alleging injuries on the vaccine injury table made up the majority of claims filed in the first decade of the program, today— after the addition of new vaccines, particularly influenza vaccine, to the table without associated injuries—the majority of the claims filed involve off-table injuries. Stakeholders report that the program has an adversarial environment, as petitioners are required to demonstrate a covered vaccine caused the injury on their VICP claim when there are no associated injuries on the table. The extent to which this will change if HHS updates the vaccine injury table to include more injuries, as expected, is yet to be seen. Second, most of the compensated cases are now adjudicated through negotiated settlement, rather than contested decisions before the special master. And while the vaccines covered by the program are included because they are recommended for children, many of the program's petitioners in recent years are adults who received covered vaccines.

Addressing one criticism of the program by stakeholders—specifically the need to increase the statute of limitations—would require a statutory change in the program. Regardless of whether the statute of limitations is increased,

HHS's efforts to increase awareness of the availability of the program will be important to help ensure that potential petitioners are aware of the program and can file claims in time. While HHS has recently taken or planned steps to improve its outreach activities, what effect, if any, these efforts will have remains to be seen. As the agency moves forward, it will be important for HRSA to identify which activities are reaching its target audiences.

AGENCY COMMENTS

We provided a draft of this report to HHS, DOJ, USCFC, and Treasury. HHS and USCFC agreed with our findings. In its comments, HHS emphasized that it administers VICP jointly with DOJ and USCFC, with HHS responsible for reviewing petitioners' claims, providing recommendations for entitlement to compensation, and making payments to petitioners and attorneys. In commenting on our identification of its efforts on VICP outreach, HHS noted that it is strengthening its outreach efforts by implementing its fiscal year 2015 VICP outreach plan, which increases outreach to target populations and includes performance measures. In its written comments, USCFC noted that the Administrative Office of the United States Courts and USCFC both supply administrative support to the Office of Special Masters and VICP without reimbursement from the trust fund. The court also commented that, while considerable strides have been made in reducing the average processing time for claims in recent years, the climbing and changing nature of the caseload, coupled with the statutory cap on the number of special masters, present a continuing challenge to the Office of Special Masters' ability to continue to reduce average processing times. USCFC also commented that following omnibus proceedings, claims have been resolved more expeditiously in recent years, and often through settlements. USCFC also commented that the Office of Special Masters strives to resolve all cases fairly and expeditiously. HHS, USCFC, DOJ, and Treasury also provided technical comments that were incorporated, as appropriate.

Sincerely yours,
Marcia Crosse
Director, Health Care

APPENDIX I: VACCINE INJURY TABLE, SEPTEMBER 2014

Vaccine	Injury[a]	Time period[b]
Vaccines against tetanus (e.g., DTaP, DTP, DT, Td, or TT)	Anaphylaxis or anaphylactic shock Brachial neuritis	4 hours 2-28 days
Vaccines against pertussis (e.g., DTP, DTaP, P, DTP-Hib)	Anaphylaxis or anaphylactic shock Encephalopathy (or encephalitis)	4 hours 72 hours
Vaccines against measles, mumps, rubella in any combination (e.g., MMR, MR, M, R)	Anaphylaxis or anaphylactic shock Encephalopathy (or encephalitis)	4 hours 5-15 days
Vaccines against measles (e.g., MMR, MR, M)	Thrombocytopenic purpura Vaccine-strain measles viral infection in an immunodeficient recipient	7-30 days 6 months
Vaccines against rubella (e.g., MMR, MR, R)	Chronic arthritis	7-42 days
Vaccines against polio (polio live virus-containing (OPV))	Paralytic Polio	
	—In a nonimmunodeficient recipient	30 days
	—In an immunodeficient recipient	6 months
	—In a vaccine-associated community case	Not applicable
	Vaccine-strain polio viral infection	
	—In a nonimmunodeficient recipient	30 days
	—In an immunodeficient recipient	6 months
	—In a vaccine-associated community case	Not applicable
Vaccines against polio (polio inactivated virus-containing (IPV))	Anaphylaxis or anaphylactic shock	4 hours

Vaccine	Injury[a]	Time period[b]
Vaccines against hepatitis B	Anaphylaxis or anaphylactic shock	4 hours
Vaccines against hemophilus influenzae type b (Hib conjugate vaccine)	No condition specified	Not applicable
Vaccines against varicella	No condition specified	Not applicable
Vaccines against rotavirusa	No condition specified	Not applicable
Vaccines against pneumococcal disease (pneumococcal conjugate vaccine)a	No condition specified	Not applicable
Vaccines against hepatitis Aa	No condition specified	Not applicable
Vaccines against influenza (trivalent vaccine)a,c	No condition specified	Not applicable
Vaccines against meningococcal diseasea	No condition specified	Not applicable
Vaccines against human papillomavirus (HPV)	No condition specified	Not applicable

Source: GAO summary of information from the Health Resources and Services Administration. | GAO-15-142

Notes: In addition to the specific vaccines currently listed on the table, the National Vaccine Injury Compensation Program (VICP) also covers new vaccines recommended by the Centers for Disease Control and Prevention for routine administration to children after publication by the Secretary of a notice of coverage, effective on the date of an applicable excise tax.

[a]This column includes the illness, disability, injury, or condition covered by the program. In addition, covered injuries include any acute complication or sequela (including death) of the listed injuries (for all but the Hib, varicella, rotavirus, pneumococcal conjugate, hepatitis A, trivalent influenza, meningococcal, and HPV vaccines).

[b]For first symptom, onset, or aggravation of injury after vaccination.

[c]Trivalent influenza vaccine was added to the table effective July 1, 2005. All additional seasonal influenza vaccines, including quadrivalent vaccine, are covered by VICP, effective November 12, 2013.

APPENDIX II: COVERED VACCINES AND INJURIES ON THE VACCINE INJURY TABLE, FISCAL YEARS 1999-2014

Vaccine	1999	2000	2001	2002	2003	2004	2005	2006	2007	2008	2009	2010	2011	2012	2013	2014[a]
Vaccines and Injuries Added to the Table before Fiscal Year 1999																
Tetanus-containing	●	●	●	●	●	●	●	●	●	●	●	●	●	●	●	●
Pertussis-containing	●	●	●	●	●	●	●	●	●	●	●	●	●	●	●	●
Measles, mumps, rubella in any combination	●	●	●	●	●	●	●	●	●	●	●	●	●	●	●	●
Measles-containing	●	●	●	●	●	●	●	●	●	●	●	●	●	●	●	●
Rubella-containing	●	●	●	●	●	●	●	●	●	●	●	●	●	●	●	●
Polio live virus-containing	●	●	●	●	●	●	●	●	●	●	●	●	●	●	●	●
Polio inactivated virus-containing	●	●	●	●	●	●	●	●	●	●	●	●	●	●	●	●
Hepatitis B	●	●	●	●	●	●	●	●	●	●	●	●	●	●	●	●
Hemophilus influenza type b (Hib) conjugate[b]	○	○	○	○	○	○	○	○	○	○	○	○	○	○	○	○
Varicella[b]	○	○	○	○	○	○	○	○	○	○	○	○	○	○	○	○
Vaccines and Injuries Added and Proposed to be Added to the Table During and After Fiscal Year 1999																
Rotavirus[c]	○	○	○	○	○	○	○	○	○	○	○	○	○	○	◐c	◐c

Vaccine	1999	2000	2001	2002	2003	2004	2005	2006	2007	2008	2009	2010	2011	2012	2013	2014[a]
Pneumococcal conjugate	—	○[d]	○	○	○	○	○	○	○	○	○	○	○	○	○	○
Hepatitis A	—	—	—	—	—	—	○	○	○	○	○	○	○	○	○	○
Trivalent influenza[e]	—	—	—	—	—	—	○	○	○	○	○	○	○	○	○	○
Meningococcal	—	—	—	—	—	—	—	—	○	○	○	○	○	○	○	○
Human Papillomavirus	—	—	—	—	—	—	—	—	○	○	○	○	○	○	○	○
Vaccines and Injuries Added and Removed from the Table since Fiscal Year 1999																
Hib polysaccharide (unconjugated)	●	●	●	●	—	—	—	—	—	—	—	—	—	—	—	—
Rotavirus rhesus-based	—	—	—	●	●	●	●	●	●	●	●	—	—	—	—	—

Legend:

●= at least one injury specified for this vaccine on the table at any point during the fiscal year

◐= HHS issued a proposed rule to add an injury to the table during the fiscal year

○= there are no table injuries specified for this vaccine

— = the vaccine is not on the table

Notes: When no injury is identified or specified for the vaccine, the petitioner must prove that the injury was caused by the vaccine. In addition to the vaccines listed on the table, the National Vaccine Injury Compensation Program (VICP) may also cover any new vaccines that are recommended by the Centers for Disease Control and Prevention's for routine administration to children and which are subject to an excise tax, but are not yet specifically listed on the vaccine injury table.

[a]The information in this column is up to date as of September 17, 2014.

[b]Hemophilus influenza type b conjugate and varicella vaccines were added to the table effective August 6, 1997.

[c]Rotavirus was added to the table effective October 22, 1998. HHS issued a proposed rule on July 24, 2013, to add an injury to the table associated with rotavirus vaccine. However, the rule was not finalized before the end of fiscal year 2014.

[d]Pneumococcal conjugate vaccine was added to the table effective December 18, 1999.

[e]Trivalent influenza vaccine was added to the table effective July 1, 2005. All additional seasonal influenza vaccines, including quadrivalent vaccine, are covered by VICP, effective November 12, 2013.

APPENDIX III: COMPENSATION TO PETITIONERS AND ATTORNEYS' FEES AND COSTS, FISCAL YEARS 1999-2013

This appendix shows the total amount paid in compensation to petitioners under the National Vaccine Injury Compensation Program and the number of compensated claims in fiscal years 1999-2013 (see table 2). It also shows the amounts the program paid in attorneys' fees and costs for those same fiscal years (see table 3).

Table 2. Compensation to Petitioners under the National Vaccine Injury Compensation Program, Fiscal Years 1999-2013

Fiscal year	Petitioners' award amount	Number of compensated claims
1999	$95,917,681	96
2000	$125,945,196	136
2001	$105,878,633	97
2002	$59,799,604	80
2003	$82,816,240	65
2004	$61,933,764	57
2005	$55,065,797	64
2006	$48,746,163	68
2007	$91,449,434	82
2008	$75,716,552	141
2009	$74,142,491	131
2010	$179,387,341	173
2011	$216,319,428	251
2012	$163,511,999	250
2013	$254,666,327	375
Total	$1,691,296,649	2,066

Source: HRSA Data and Statistics Report, August 1, 2014. | GAO-15-142

Table 3. Payments to Attorneys under the National Vaccine Injury Compensation Program, Fiscal Years 1999-2013

Fiscal year	Compensated attorneys' fees/cost payments	Dismissed attorneys' fees/cost payments	Interim attorneys' fees/cost payments	Number of payments to attorneys
1999	$2,799,911	$2,306,957	$0.00	213
2000	$4,112,369	$1,724,451	$0.00	216
2001	$3,373,866	$2,066,225	$0.00	154

Fiscal year	Compensated attorneys' fees/cost payments	Dismissed attorneys' fees/cost payments	Interim attorneys' fees/cost payments	Number of payments to attorneys
2002	$2,653,599	$656,245	$0.00	130
2003	$3,147,755	$1,545,655	$0.00	134
2004	$3,079,329	$1,198,616	$0.00	126
2005	$2,694,664	$1,790,587	$0.00	135
2006	$2,441,199	$1,353,633	$0.00	122
2007	$4,034,154	$1,692,020	$0.00	143
2008	$5,191,771	$2,511,313	$117,265	216
2009	$5,404,712	$1,557,140	$4,241,363	195
2010	$5,961,744	$1,886,240	$1,978,804	251
2011	$9,572,043	$5,589,417	$2,001,771	682
2012	$9,104,489	$8,621,182	$5,420,258	1,304
2013	$13,333,180	$6,970,279	$1,454,852	1,128
Total	$76,904,784	$41,469,960	$15,214,312	5,149

Source: HRSA Data and Statistics Report, August 1, 2014. | GAO-15-142

End Notes

[1] In this report, we use the term injury to refer to an illness, disability, or similar condition.

[2] VICP was established by the National Childhood Vaccine Injury Act of 1986. Pub. L. No. 99-660, title III, §§ 301 et seq., 100 Stat. 3743, 3755 (amending the Public Health Service Act by inserting a new title XXI; codified, as amended, at 42 U.S.C. 300aa-1 et seq.).

[3] Petitions may also be filed for compensation for deaths from vaccines covered by the program.

[4] GAO, *Vaccine Injury Compensation Program Challenged to Settle Claims Quickly and Easily*, GAO/HEHS-00-8 (Washington, D.C.: Dec. 22, 1999).

[5] For the purposes of this report, we use the term claim to refer to the petition and case filed under VICP. We refer to the individuals filing the claims as petitioners. HRSA administers the program in conjunction with DOJ and USCFC.

[6] We examined USCFC data showing when VICP petitions were filed and when each claim was adjudicated for petitions filed from fiscal year 1999 through March 31, 2014.

[7] The Advisory Commission on Childhood Vaccines (ACCV) consists of nine members appointed by the Secretary of Health and Human Services and advises the Secretary on certain issues relating to VICP. See 42 U.S.C. § 300aa-19. Some individual members of the ACCV provided GAO with their personal views that do not necessarily reflect the official position of the ACCV, which is reflected in consensus recommendations made by the ACCV to the Secretary of HHS.

[8] The term obligation refers to a definite commitment by a federal agency that creates a legal liability to make payments immediately or in the future. We examined agency data on obligations for full-time equivalent (FTE) staff, and for other expenses.

[9] The stakeholders we contacted included the National Vaccine Information Center, Vaccine Injured Petitioners' Bar Association, American Academy of Family Physicians, and

American Academy of Pediatrics. In addition, other individuals and organizations contacted GAO and provided comments, which we considered as we conducted our review.

[10] Petitioners must first file a VICP claim before suing in civil court unless the civil suit is for $1,000 or less. 42 U.S.C. § 300aa-11(a)(2)(A).

[11] The program may provide compensation for individuals who were injured or died after receiving the covered vaccines regardless of their age at the time of vaccination—that is, even though the vaccines are recommended for routine administration for children, adults who are vaccinated with a covered vaccine are also eligible for the program.

[12] 42 U.S.C §§ 300aa-11(c)(1), 300aa-13(a)(1). A petitioner's claim of an on-table injury must also meet the Qualifications and Aids for Interpretation that define the injuries listed on the vaccine injury table.

[13] The preponderance of evidence standard is generally interpreted to require that the party with the burden of persuasion—here, that party is the petitioner—must establish that a fact in question is more likely true than not. See 29 Am. Jur. 2d Evid. § 173. This standard is used for VICP claims in a manner similar to its use in civil court but without regard to fault.

[14] The agency must provide for notice and opportunity for a public hearing and at least 180 days of public comment, as well as provide the Advisory Commission on Childhood Vaccines at least 90 days to provide recommendations and comment on proposed rules to modify the table.

[15] 42 U.S.C. § 300aa-14(e). The effective date for a vaccine added to the vaccine injury table is the effective date of an excise tax on the vaccine. The Omnibus Budget Reconciliation Act of 1993. Pub. L. No. 103-66 § 13632 (a)(3), 107 Stat. 312, 646 (codified at 42 U.S.C. § 300aa-14 note). When a new vaccine or a new injury is added to the vaccine injury table, claims that do not meet the general filing deadlines must be filed within 2 years from the date the vaccine or injury is added to the table for injuries or deaths that occurred up to 8 years before the table change.

[16] Pub. L. No. 99-660, § 311(a), 100 Stat. 3771 (codified as amended at 42 U.S.C. § 300aa-19).

[17] GAO/HEHS-00-8.

[18] Individuals eligible to file a VICP claim include the person who sustained the vaccine-related injury or that person's legal representative if that person is a child, disabled, or deceased. 42 U.S.C. § 300aa-11(b)(1)(A).

[19] See 42 U.S.C. § 300aa-16.

[20] The Office of Special Masters is an office within the USCFC, part of the judiciary, comprising up to eight court-appointed special masters who develop expertise in vaccine-injury claims. According to the Office of Special Masters, most claims are assigned to special masters on a random basis, but to the extent that a special master has acquired expertise in a specific injury or vaccine, claims may be directed to a particular special master.

[21] A special master may suspend activity on a claim while waiting for additional documentation.

[22] Even when HHS concedes a case or a case is settled, the USCFC issues a decision and judgment awarding compensation. A claim is not compensated if the court determines the petitioner is not entitled to compensation or in certain other circumstances, such as where the petitioner elects not to receive compensation or withdraws the petition.

[23] According to HRSA, such a settlement is not an admission by HHS that the vaccine caused the petitioner's alleged injuries, and in settlements, the court does not determine that the vaccine caused the injury. See Health Resources and Services Administration, Statistics Report-August 1, 2014, http://www.hrsa.gov/vaccinecompensation/statisticsreport.pdf, p. 9, accessed Sept. 8, 2014. Once a settlement is reached, it must be formally approved by the decision of the special master, provided the special master determines it is reasonable.

[24] If the special master rules that a petitioner is not entitled to compensation, the petitioner may request to have the decision reviewed by a judge of the USCFC who may issue a decision in favor of the petitioner. HHS may appeal the decision of the special master if the petitioner is awarded compensation.

[25] Damages may be agreed to by the parties, or the special master may hold another hearing or rule upon the record without conducting a hearing.

[26] Attorney fees and costs may be paid if the court determines there is a reasonable basis for the petition and the petition was filed in good faith. These payments generally reflect the actual time and expense devoted to the case.

[27] See 42 U.S.C. § 300aa-21(a).

[28] The Vaccine Injury Compensation Trust Fund is funded by a $0.75 excise tax on each dose of vaccine recommended by HHS's Centers for Disease Control and Prevention for routine administration to children. The excise tax is imposed on each disease that is prevented in a vaccine. Influenza vaccine, for example, is taxed $0.75 because it prevents one disease; measles-mumps-rubella vaccine, which prevents three diseases, is taxed $2.25. The trust fund receives net revenues from the excise tax, plus interest on investments in government securities.

[29] Within USCFC, only the Office of Special Masters receives appropriations from the trust fund.

[30] The Chief Special Master is responsible to provide for the efficient, expeditious, and effective handling of petitions under VICP. 41 U.S.C. § 300aa-12(c)(6).

[31] See 42 U.S.C. § 300aa-26.

[32] 42 U.S.C. § 300aa-10(c).

[33] USCFC data on processing times for claims runs from the time the petition was filed until judgment was entered.

[34] Of the claims filed since fiscal year 2009 that were adjudicated as of March 31, 2014, the claim that took the shortest time to adjudicate took 3 days, and the claim that took the longest time to adjudicate took 1,981 days (nearly 5 and a half years).

[35] Performance measures, including a measure for average claims processing time, were developed for VICP during the Program Assessment Rating Tool review conducted by the Office of Management and Budget for the fiscal year 2007 budget. HHS reports the targets and tracks the program's performance for average claims processing time in HRSA's annual congressional budget justifications.

[36] Altarum Institute, *Determining the Feasibility of Evaluating the National Vaccine Injury Compensation Program, Final Report,* a report prepared for the Health Resources and Services Administration, June 15, 2009. Of 716 petitioners the researchers identified as meeting their inclusion criteria,107 responded to their survey and 103 responded to this question on the length of the process. The results of this study cannot be generalized to the population of all petitioners who completed the VICP process; instead, they reflect only the VICP petitioners who responded to the survey. According to HRSA, petitioners were included in the sample if they (1) had filed a claim that had been compensated or dismissed in fiscal years 2004-2008 and (2) were represented by an attorney.

[37] If a special master fails to make a decision on a petition within 240 days (excluding any period of suspension), or if USCFC fails to enter a judgment on a petition within 420 days after the date on which the petition was filed (excluding any period of suspension), petitioners can withdraw their claim from VICP. 42 U.S.C. § 300aa-12(g). While USCFC officials report that most claims exceed both the 240-day and the 420-day limits when periods of suspension are not excluded, USCFC does not track suspensions so available data do not

show how much time a case was suspended and how many cases met the statutory time frames.

[38] Petitioners are required by statute to submit their supporting documentation or evidence at the time they file their petition. See 42 U.S.C. § 300aa-11(c)(2). According to DOJ, petitions are frequently filed without documentation, which delays adjudication.

[39] Special masters report allowing these delays in order to accumulate sufficient evidence to adjudicate a claim, but they could not provide a precise number.

[40] See Health Resources and Services Administration, Statistics Report-October 2, 2014, http://www.hrsa.gov/vaccinecompensation/statisticsreport.pdf, accessed October 8, 2014.

[41] The omnibus autism proceeding was the largest of several instances in which the courts addressed groupings of similar claims. Since 1999, the USCFC has grouped similar claims to manage hepatitis B vaccine injury claims, claims alleging an injury of type 1 diabetes, and claims that certain childhood vaccinations have caused or contributed to autism. According to the Office of Special Masters, the omnibus autism proceeding was the largest of these groupings, involving over 5,000 claims, with the hepatitis B grouping involving several hundred and the type 1 diabetes grouping involving fewer than 50 claims.

[42] According to the Office of Special Masters, petitioners withdrew a third theory of causation.

[43] See 42 U.S.C. § 300aa-21(b). By filing a "Short-Form Autism Petition for Vaccine Compensation," a petitioner could elect to be part of the Omnibus Autism Proceeding and simultaneously choose to stay his or her case-specific proceeding on his own petition until the conclusion of the Omnibus Autism Proceeding. See Office of Special Masters, Autism General Order #1, July 3, 2002 (http://www.uscfc.uscourts.gov/sites/default/files/autism/Autism+General+Order1.pdf), accessed October 14, 2014.

[44] See In Re: Claims for Vaccine Injuries Resulting in Autism Spectrum Disorder or a Similar Neurodevelopmental Disorder, Fed. Cl. Spec. Mstr. Update, p. 3, Jan. 12, 2011 (indicating that proceedings in all test cases had concluded and that decisions in all such cases rejected petitioners' theories of causation).

[45] According to the Office of Special Masters, these petitioners proceeded on other theories of causation.

[46] Although the rhesus-based rotavirus vaccine was added to the table with an associated injury in 2002, it was removed in 2008. See 67 Fed. Reg. 48558 (Jul. 25, 2002) (addition to table); 73 Fed. Reg. 59528 (Oct. 9, 2008) (removal from table).

[47] In October 1999, the Centers for Disease Control and Prevention recommended the hepatitis A vaccine be administered to children in states, counties, and communities with rates of hepatitis A that were twice the 1987-1997 national average or greater. However, the hepatitis A vaccine was not covered by VICP until 2004, when the American Jobs Creation Act of 2004 imposed an excise tax for all hepatitis A vaccines. Pub. L. No. 108- 357, § 889(a), 118 Stat. 1418, 1643 (codified at 26 U.S.C. § 4132(a)(I)).

[48] In addition to the rhesus-based rotavirus vaccine, which was removed in 2008, unconjugated Hemophilus influenza type b (Hib) polysaccharide vaccine was removed from the vaccine injury table in 2002. See 67 Fed. Reg. 48558 (Jul. 25, 2002).

[49] There were two vaccines on the table prior to fiscal year 1999 that had no covered injuries listed: Hemophilus influenza type b (Hib) vaccine (which prevents meningitis and other serious infections) and varicella vaccine (which prevents chicken pox).

[50] HHS has also been considering adding injuries in association to covered vaccines that already have associated injuries on the vaccine injury table.

[51] 78 Fed. Reg. 44512 (Jul. 24, 2013) (to be codified at 42 U.S.C. § 100.3).

[52] In 2009, HHS commissioned the Institute of Medicine to review specific injuries in association with vaccines that are currently on the table. These vaccines include varicella; influenza, hepatitis B; human papillomavirus; measles, mumps, and rubella; hepatitis A; meningococcal; and vaccines containing tetanus. See Institute of Medicine, *Adverse Effects of Vaccines: Evidence and Causality* (Washington, D.C.: The National Academies Press: 2012).

[53] HRSA officials said they are also considering changes in the language defining injuries on the table.

[54] Public hearings on the proposed rule for adding intussusception as a covered injury associated with the rotavirus vaccine took place on January 13, 2014, and April 28, 2014.

[55] Health Resources and Services Administration, *Justification of Estimates to Appropriations Committees*, Fiscal Year 2013, accessed November 4, 2014 http://www.hrsa.gov/about/budget/budgetjustification2013.pdf.

[56] GAO/HEHS-00-8.

[57] The five vaccines included hepatitis A, human pappilomavirus, influenza, meningococcal, and pneumococcal conjugate vaccines. According to HRSA data, 1,245 claims filed since fiscal year 2005, including claims filed as part of the Omnibus Autism Proceeding, did not specify a vaccine and 30 claims specified a nonqualified vaccine— that is, a vaccine not covered under VICP.

[58] Vaccines generally recommended for adults (as well as children) and currently covered by VICP include vaccines to protect against influenza, tetanus, diphtheria, pertussis, varicella, human papillomavirus, pneumococcal disease (pneumococcal conjugate vaccine), measles, mumps, and rubella. See http://www.cdc.gov/vaccines/schedules/downloads/adult/adult-schedule-easy-read-bw.pdf, accessed Oct. 9, 2014.

[59] According to HRSA data, 5,377 claims filed since fiscal year 1999 (as of March 31, 2014) did not specify which covered vaccine caused an alleged injury and 57 claims specified a vaccine not covered by the program.

[60] In this report, investments in U.S. securities issued by the Bureau of Fiscal Service and the fund balance with Treasury comprise the balance of the trust fund at the end of the fiscal year.

[61] Net revenue from vaccine excise taxes and interest on investments comprise income for the trust fund. Disbursements to HRSA—for compensation to petitioners, attorneys' fees and costs, and administrative expenses, and to DOJ and the USCFC for the Office of Special Masters—for expenses associated with processing National Vaccine Injury Compensation Program (VICP) claims, comprise disbursements from the trust fund.

[62] See 26 U.S.C. § 9602.

[63] There is no cap on the amount of an award in a vaccine injury case, but the law does provide certain restrictions, such as a prohibition on punitive damages and limits on pain and suffering and emotional distress. Awards may include compensation for actual and anticipated loss of earnings. In some cases, compensation may be provided in the form of an annuity. In the event of a vaccine-related death, VICP will award $250,000 to the estate of the deceased. See 42 U.S.C.§ 300aa–15. Injury-related damages in addition to the statutory death benefit may be awarded.

[64] Attorneys are prohibited from taking a contingent fee on compensation awarded to a petitioner. 42 U.S.C. § 300aa-15(e).

[65] According to the Office of Special Masters, interim awards are made at the special master's discretion, depending on a variety of factors, including but not limited to the duration of the litigation (e.g., lengthy proceedings), the stage of the proceedings, the amounts sought (e.g.,

demonstrating that substantial costs have been incurred), and the documented need for an interim award (e.g., demonstrating undue hardship).

[66] The total obligation to each agency may not match the amount that Treasury reported it disbursed from the trust fund during a given fiscal year because the agencies' obligations for petitioners' compensation, attorneys' fees, and other expenses associated with the program do not always occur in the same fiscal year that Treasury disburses funding to the agencies.

[67] Altarum Institute, *Determining the Feasibility of Evaluating the National Vaccine Injury Compensation Program*. HRSA contracted for this study in 2005, which surveyed petitioners regarding their perceptions of access to VICP information, program implementation and processes, financial award decision, and overall satisfaction. According to HRSA, petitioners were included in the sample if they (1) had filed a claim that had been compensated or dismissed in fiscal years 2004-2008 and (2) were represented by an attorney. Of 716 petitioners the researchers identified as meeting their inclusion criteria, 107 responded to their survey.

[68] In each of HRSA's annual justification of estimates for appropriations committees for fiscal years 2011-2014, HRSA noted that the agency has been criticized for not adequately promoting public awareness of the VICP.

[69] Division of Vaccine Injury Compensation, *National Vaccine Injury Compensation Program Strategic Plan* (April 2006).

[70] Banyan Communications, Inc., *The Comprehensive National Vaccine Injury Compensation Program Marketing and Outreach Communication Plan*, a report prepared for the Health Resources and Services Administration, (Nov. 2010).

[71] According to HRSA officials, the agency has been implementing some of the activities recommended in the November 2010 plans since that plan was issued, but the agency did not formally document its outreach efforts until the fiscal year 2014 VICP outreach plan. Agency officials report that the 2014 plan was developed because HRSA is taking a more strategic approach to its outreach and wanted to formally document these efforts.

[72] As part of its fiscal year 2011 budget justification, HRSA reported that exhibiting at conferences had proven beneficial in increasing knowledge of the availability of the program and that it planned exhibiting at medical and legal conferences in fiscal year 2011.

[73] The current statute of limitations, in general, requires that claims be filed within 3 years of the date of the first symptom or manifestation of the onset or significant aggravation of an injury and within 2 years of a death (and within 4 years of the date of the first symptom or manifestation of the onset or significant aggravation of the injury from which a death resulted). Generally, when a vaccine or injury is added to the vaccine injury table, petitioners are required to file claims within 2 years from the date the vaccine or injury is added to the table for injuries or deaths that occurred up to 8 years before the table change. See 42 U.S.C. § 300aa-16.

[74] HHS has proposed extending the statutory time limits for filing a VICP claim in the past. For example, in commenting on a draft of our 1999 report, the department stated that the legislative proposals it had sent to the Congress included doubling the statutory time limit for filing a claim. GAO/HEHS-00-8, 39. DOJ officials also reported they believed their department had supported previous proposals to extend the program's statute of limitations.

In: National Vaccine Injury Compensation ... ISBN: 978-1-63482-528-3
Editor: Preston Torres

Chapter 2

WHAT YOU NEED TO KNOW ABOUT THE NATIONAL VACCINE INJURY COMPENSATION PROGRAM*

Health Resources and Services Administration

NOTE

What You Need to Know About the National Vaccine Injury Compensation Program (VICP) is not a legal document. The official provisions are contained in the relevant laws, regulations and Court decisions. Because this provides only general information, you may wish to consult a lawyer.

WHAT IS THE NATIONAL VACCINE INJURY COMPENSATION PROGRAM (VICP)?

Vaccines save lives by preventing disease in the people who receive them. Most people who get vaccines have no serious problems. However, vaccines, like any medicines, can rarely cause serious problems, such as severe allergic reactions. In those rare cases, the VICP, which is a Federal program, provides

* This is an edited, reformatted and augmented version of a document issued by the U.S. Department of Health and Human Services, December 2011.

compensation to people found to be injured by certain vaccines. The U.S. Court of Federal Claims decides who will be paid. Three Federal government offices have a role in the VICP:

- the U.S. Department of Health and Human Services (HHS);
- the U.S. Department of Justice (DOJ); and
- the U.S. Court of Federal Claims (the Court).

The VICP is located in the HHS, Health Resources and Services Administration, Healthcare Systems Bureau, Division of Vaccine Injury Compensation.

Why and When Was the VICP Created?

In the early 1980s, news reports of serious side effects from the DTP (diphtheria, tetanus, pertussis) vaccine caused some to question the safety of the vaccine. Parents began filing many lawsuits against vaccine companies, doctors, and nurses. Some vaccine companies decided to stop making vaccines, which created vaccine shortages and threatened the Nation's health.

All of these problems led a group of doctors, public health organizations, vaccine companies and private citizens to encourage Congress to enact a new law to compensate those found to be injured by childhood vaccines. The National Childhood Vaccine Injury Act of 1986 (Public Law 99-660) created the VICP, which began on October 1, 1988.

What Vaccines Are Covered by the VICP?

- Diphtheria, tetanus, pertussis (DTP, DTaP, Tdap, DT, Td, or TT)
- Haemophilus influenzae type b (Hib)
- Hepatitis A (HAV)
- Hepatitis B (HBV)
- Human papillomavirus (HPV)
- Influenza (TIV, LAIV) [given each year]
- Measles, mumps, rubella (MMR, MR, M, R)
- Meningococcal (MCV4, MPSV4)
- Polio (OPV or IPV)

- Pneumococcal conjugate (PCV)
- Rotavirus (RV)
- Varicella (VZV)
- Any combination of the vaccines above
- Additional vaccines may be added in the future

For a description of the diseases prevented by these vaccines, see page 15 in the Appendix.

How Does the VICP Work?

First, a claim must be filed by or on the behalf of the individual thought to be injured by a vaccine covered by the VICP. A claim is started by filing a legal document called a petition that is prepared by you or your lawyer to request compensation under the VICP. Anyone who files a claim is called a petitioner. The only form required is the Court's cover sheet for the claim. You may obtain a copy of the cover sheet and a sample claim by calling (202) 357-6400. Your claim should address the following information:

- who was injured by the vaccine;
- which vaccine caused the injury;
- when the vaccine was given;
- the city and State or country where the vaccine was given;
- the type of injury;
- when the first symptom of the injury appeared; and
- how long the effects of the injury lasted.

Your claim should also include your medical records and/or other appropriate documents, the Court's cover sheet, and the $400.00 filing fee. If you are unable to pay this fee, call (202) 357-6400 for assistance.

One copy should be sent to:
Director, Division of Vaccine Injury Compensation
HRSA, Healthcare Systems Bureau
Parklawn Building, Room 11C-26
5600 Fishers Lane
Rockville, Maryland 20857

Who May File a Claim?

- You may file a claim if you received a vaccine covered by the VICP and believe that you have been injured by this vaccine.
- You may also file a claim if you are a parent or legal guardian of a child or disabled adult who received a vaccine covered by the VICP and believe that the person was injured by this vaccine.
- You may file a claim if you are the legal representative of the estate of a deceased person who received a vaccine covered by the VICP and believe that the person's death resulted from the vaccine injury.
- You may file a claim if you are ***not*** a United States citizen.
- Some people who receive vaccines outside of the U.S. may be eligible for compensation. The vaccines must have been covered by the VICP and given in the following circumstances:
  - the injured person must have received a vaccine in the U.S. trust territories; or
  - if the vaccine was administered outside of the U.S. or its trust territories: 1) the injured person must have been a U.S. citizen serving in the military or a U.S. government employee, or have been a dependent of such a citizen; or 2) the injured person must have received a vaccine manufactured by a vaccine company located in the U.S. and returned to the U.S. within 6 months after the date of vaccination.

In addition, to be eligible to file a claim, the effects of the person's injury must have: 1) lasted for more than 6 months after the vaccine was given; or 2) resulted in a hospital stay *and* surgery; or 3) resulted in death.

What Medical Records and Other Documents Are Requested to Ensure a Timely Review of My Claim?

You must include certain medical records and/or other appropriate documents with the claim. If some medical records are unavailable, you must identify those records and explain why they are unavailable. The medical review and processing of the claim may be delayed if you do not include the appropriate medical records and other documents with the claim.

In order to ensure that your claim is processed in a timely manner, the VICP suggests that you include the following medical records and other documents when filing your claim with the Court and the Secretary of Health and Human Services, c/o Director, Division of Vaccine Injury Compensation.

Medical Records

1.* Prenatal and Birth Records

- Mother's prenatal record
- Delivery record
- Birth Certificate
- Newborn hospital record including doctors'/nurses' notes, and radiology/lab results
- Any hospitalization face sheet with final diagnosis

2. Medical Records Prior to Vaccination

- Clinic notes (such as Well Baby visits)
- Private doctor visits
- Growth charts/lab/radiology results
- Consultation reports and evaluations
- Developmental charts

3. Vaccination Record (if available)

- Lot number
- Manufacturer

4. Post-Injury Hospital/Emergency Treatment Records

- Admission/discharge summaries
- History and physical records
- Progress notes (including doctors'/nurses' notes)
- Medication records
- Lab/radiology/EEG results
- Flow sheets (respiratory care/treatments)
- Consultation reports and evaluations

5. Post-Injury Outpatient Records

- History and physical records
- Progress notes (including doctors'/nurses' notes)

- Medication records
- Lab/radiology/EEG results
- Clinic notes
- All evaluations

6. Vaccine Adverse Event Reporting System (VAERS) Form (If Submitted)

7. Long Term Records (That Apply to Your Injury)

- School records
- Consultation reports and evaluations
- Educational testing records
- Psychological testing records
- Police/ambulance records

8. Death Records (If Applicable)

- Death Certificate
- Autopsy report (if done)
- Autopsy slides

*Note: Number 1 may be omitted if the injured person is an adult.

Do I Need a Lawyer to File a Claim?

You do not need a lawyer to file a claim. However, since this is a legal process, most people use a lawyer. If certain minimal requirements are met, the VICP will pay your lawyer's fees and other legal costs related to your claim, whether or not you are paid for a vaccine injury or death. The VICP will not pay the fees of petitioners representing themselves, but will pay their other legal costs, whether or not the claim is paid as long as certain minimal requirements are met.

What Are the Deadlines to File a Claim?

The general filing deadlines are:

- For an *injury,*your claim must be filed within 3 years after the first symptom of the vaccine injury.
- For a *death,*your claim must be filed within 2 years of the death and 4 years after the start of first symptom of the vaccine-related injury from which the death occurred.

When a *new vaccine* is covered by the VICP or when a *new injury/condition* is added to the Vaccine Injury Table (Table), claims that do not meet the general filing deadlines must be filed within 2 years from the date the vaccine or injury/condition is added to the Table for i njuries or deaths that occurred up to 8 years before the Table change. The Table lists and explains injuries that are presumed to be caused by vaccines. For more details about the Table, visit *www.hrsa.gov/vaccinecompensation.*

For example, the hepatitis A vaccine was covered by the VICP as of December 1, 2004. Under the general filing deadline for an injury, the claim must be filed within 3 years after the first symptom of the vaccine injury. However, claims that do not meet the general filing deadlines must be filed by December 1 , 2006 for injuries or deaths that occurred on or after December 1,1996.

What Is the Process for Filing a Claim?

A summary of the claims process is provided below. The Court has documents that explain the process in more detail. To obtain these documents, you may visit the Court's Web site at *www.uscfc.uscourts.gov* or call (202) 357-6400.Most petitioners use a lawyer

since this is a legal process, and the Rules of the Court are very specific and must be followed.

The process for filing a claim is:

1. the petitioner or petitioner's lawyer sends one original and two copies of the claim along with the medical records, other appropriate documents and a $400.00 filing fee to the Court;
2. the petitioner or petitioner's lawyer sends one copy of the claim including the medical records and other appropriate documents to the Secretary of Health and Human Services, c/o Director, Division of Vaccine Injury Compensation;

3. the Court sends one copy of the claim and medical records to the DOJ;
4. HHS reviews the medical information in the claim and this review is sent to the *DOJ* lawyer who represents the Secretary of Health and Human Services;
5. the *DOJ* lawyer reviews the legal aspects of the claim and writes a report;
6. the HHS and DOJ reviews are combined into one report that is sent to the Court and petitioner or petitioner's lawyer;
7. the DOJ and petitioner or petitioner's lawyer take legal action to resolve the claim;
8. a "special master" (a lawyer appointed by the judges of the Court) decides if the claim will be paid and how much will be paid for the claim;
9. if the special master decides to pay the claim, the petitioner must make a decision to accept or reject the special master's decision in writing; and
10. the special master's decision may be appealed to a judge of the Court by the petitioner or HHS, then to the U.S. Court of Appeals for the Federal Circuit and, finally, to the U.S. Supreme Court.

What Must Be Proved in Order to Be Paid?

You must prove that:

- the injured person received a vaccine listed on the Table; and
- the first symptom of the injury/condition on the Table as defined in the Qualifications and Aids to Interpretation (Aids)* occurred within the time period listed on the Table; or
- the vaccine caused the injury; or
- the vaccine caused an existing illness to get worse (significantly aggravated).

In addition, the Court must determine that the injury or death did not result from any other possible causes.

What Is the Vaccine Injury Table?

The Table makes it easier for some people to get compensation. The Table lists and explains injuries/conditions that are presumed to be caused by vaccines. It also lists time periods in which the first symptom of these injuries/conditions must occur after receiving the vaccine. If the first symptom of these injuries/conditions occur within the listed time periods, it is presumed that the vaccine was the cause of the injury or condition unless another cause is found. For example, if you received the tetanus vaccine and had a severe allergic reaction (anaphylaxis) within 4 hours after receiving the vaccine, then it is presumed that the tetanus vaccine caused the injury if no other cause is found.

If your injury/condition is not on the Table or if your injury/condition did not occur within the time period on the Table, you must prove that the vaccine caused the injury/ condition. Such proof must be based on medical records or opinion, which may include expert witness testimony.

The Table and Aids change sometimes. To obtain a copy of the latest Table and Aids, visit the VICP Website at *www.hrsa.gov/vaccine compensation,* or call 1-800-338-2382.

The following is a list of the vaccines covered by the VICP. These vaccines can be given alone or combined with other vaccines. The listing also includes the injuries/conditions associated with these vaccines and the time period in which the first symptom of these injuries/ conditions must occur in order for the VICP to presume that the vaccine was the cause. For a description of the diseases prevented by these vaccines, see page 13 in the Appendix.

Important: This is only a summary of the Table. [The definitions of these injuries/ conditions are in the Aids.]

Vaccine	Injuries/Conditions	Time Period
DIPTHERIA	See pertussis and tetanus.	
HAEMOPHILUS INFLUENZAE TYPE b (Hib)	There are no Table injuries specified for this vaccine.[1]	Not applicable
HEPATITIS A (HAV)	There are no Table injuries specified for this vaccine.[1]	Not applicable
HEPATITIS B (HBV)	A sudden, severe, and sometimes deadly allergic reaction (Anaphylaxis or Anaphylactic Shock)[2]	0-4 hours

(Continued)

Vaccine	Injuries/Conditions	Time Period
INFLUENZA	There are no Table injuries specified for this vaccine.[1]	Not applicable
MEASLES, MUMPS, RUBELLA (MMR, MR,	A sudden, severe, and sometimes deadly allergic reaction (Anaphylaxis or Anaphylactic Shock)[2]	0-4 hours
M, R)	Disorder of the brain (Encephalopathy)2	5-15 days
MEASLES (MMR, MR, MR)	A decrease in the number of platelets in the blood (Thrombocytopenic Purpura)[2]	7-30 days
	Measles virus infection in an immunodeficient person[2]	0-6 months
PERTUSSIS (DTaP, Tdap, DTP, P, DTP-Hib)	A sudden, severe, and sometimes deadly allergic reaction (Anaphylaxis or Anaphylactic Shock)2	0-4 hours
	Disorder of the brain (Encephalopathy)[2]	0-72 hours
PNEUMOCOCCAL	There are no Table injuries specified for this vaccine.[1]	Not applicable
CONJUGATE (PCV)		
POLIO INACTIVATED POLIO (IPV)	A sudden, severe, and sometimes deadly allergic reaction (Anaphylaxis or Anaphylactic Shock)[2]	0-4 hours
ORAL POLIO (OPV)3	1) Paralysis from the polio virus in the person who: • received the vaccine[2] • received the vaccine and is unable to have a normal immune response to this vaccine (immunodeficient)[2] • came in contact with a person who recently received the vaccine[2]	0-30 days 0-6 months no time limit
Vaccine	Adverse Event (Serious Side Effects)	Time Period
POLIO (continued) ORAL POLIO (OPV)[3]	2) Vaccine-strain polio infection the person who: • Received the vaccine [2] • Received the vaccine and is unable to have a normal immune response to	0-30 days 0-6 days

Vaccine	Adverse Event (Serious Side Effects)	Time Period
	this vaccine (immunodeficient)[2] • Came in contact with a person who recently received the vaccine [2]	No time limit
ROTAVIRUS (RV)	There are no Table injuries specified for this vaccine.[1]	Not applicable
RUBELLA (MMR, MR, R)	A persistent swelling of the joints (Chronic Arthritis) [2]	7-42 days
TETANUS (DTaP, Tdap, DTP-Hib, DT, Td or TT)	A sudden, severe, and sometimes deadly allergic reaction (Anaphylaxis or Anaphylactic Shock) [2] Damage to a nerve or group of nerves in the under arm (Brachial Neuritis) [2]	0-4 hours 2-28 days
VARICELLA (VZV)	There are no Table injuries specified for this vaccine.[1]	Not applicable
Human papillomavirus (HPV)	There are no Table injuries specified for this vaccine.[1]	Not applicable
Meningococcal (MCV4, MPSV4)	There are no Table injuries specified for this vaccine.[1]	Not applicable

[1] When no injury is identified or specified with this vaccine, the petitioner must prove that the injury was caused by the vaccine.

[2] In addition, any serious problems resulting from this injury/condition, including death.

[3] This vaccine is no longer given in the U.S.

What Are the Types of Payments?

For an *injury*, you may be paid:

- a reasonable amount for past and future nonreimbursable medical, custodial care, and rehabilitation costs, and related expenses (There is no limit on the amount a person with an injury may be paid for these types of expenses. Payments are based on your vaccine injury needs.);
- up to $250,000 for actual and projected pain and suffering;
- lost earnings; and/or
- reasonable lawyers' fees and other legal costs or legal costs, not fees, of petitioners representing themselves, if your claim was filed on a reasonable basis and in good faith.

For a *death*, you may be paid:

- up to $250,000 as a death benefit for the estate of the deceased; and
- reasonable lawyers' fees and other legal costs or legal costs, not fees, of petitioners representing themselves, if your claim was filed on a reasonable basis and in good faith.

Can I File a Lawsuit Outside the VICP?

Most of the time, you must first file and have your claim processed with the VICP before a civil lawsuit can be filed against the vaccine company or the person who gave the vaccine. If you would like to file a civil lawsuit outside of the VICP, contact a lawyer for advice.

What Is the Vaccine Adverse Event Reporting System (VAERS)?

VAERS is a Federal program used to report injuries or illnesses that occur after a vaccine is given. Filing a VAERS report is not the same as filing a claim with the VICP. VAERS and the VICP are different programs. For more information about VAERS, call 1-800-822-7967 or visit their Web site at *www.vaers.hhs.gov*.

How Do I Obtain More Information About the VICP?

National Vaccine Injury Compensation Program Parklawn Building, Room 11C-26
5600 Fishers Lane
Rockville, Maryland 20857; or
1-800-338-2382
www.hrsa.gov/vaccinecompensation

How Do I Obtain More Information About Filing a Claim?

Clerk
U.S. Court of Federal Claims 717 Madison Place, N.W. Washington, D.C. 20439
(202) 357-6400
www.uscfc.uscourts.gov/osmpage.htm

How Do I Obtain a List of Lawyers?

Clerk
U.S. Court of Federal Claims
717 Madison Place, N.W.
Washington, DC 20439
(202) 357-6400;
www.uscfc.uscourts.gov
or
Your State or local bar association

APPENDIX

Description of Diseases Prevented by VICP Covered Vaccines

Vaccines	Description of Diseases Prevented by Covered Vaccines
DIPTHERIA	A bacterial disease which can cause a thick covering in the back of the throat, and can lead to breathing problems, paralysis, heart failure, and even death.
HAEMOPHILUS INFLUENZAE	A bacterial disease which can cause meningitis, pneumonia,
TYPE B	severe swelling in the throat (making it hard to breathe), infections of the blood, joints, bones, and covering of the heart, and death. Meningitis is an infection of the covering of the brain.
HEPATITIS A	Hepatitis A can cause mild "flu-like" illness, jaundice, severe stomach pains and diarrhea, and can lead to a serious liver disease.

(Continued)

Vaccines	Description of Diseases Prevented by Covered Vaccines
HEPATITIS B	Hepatitis B virus can cause short term (acute) illness, and can lead to loss of appetite, diarrhea and vomiting, tiredness, jaundice (yellow skin or eyes), and pain in muscles, joints, and stomach. It can also cause long-term (chronic) illness which can lead to liver damage (cirrhosis), liver cancer and/or death.
INFLUENZA	Influenza virus can cause fever, sore throat, chills, fatigue, cough, headache, and muscle aches. It is a very contagious disease which spreads from infected persons to the nose or throat of others.
MEASLES	Measles virus can cause rash, cough, runny nose, eye irritatio which can lead to ear infection, pneumonia, seizures (jerking or staring spells) brain damage, and death.
MUMPS	Mumps virus can cause fever, headache, and swollen glands, and can lead to deafness, meningitis (infection of the brain and spinal cord covering), painful swelling of the testicles or ovaries, and, rarely, death.
PERTUSSIS (WHOOPING COUGH)	A bacterial disease which can cause coughing spells so bad that it is hard to eat, drink, or breathe, and can lead to pneumonia, seizures (jerking and staring spells), brain damage, and death. It is also called Whooping Cough.
PNEUMOCOCCAL CONJUGATE	A bacterial infection which can lead to serious illness and death, and is the leading cause of bacterial meningitis in the United States.
POLIO	Polio virus can cause paralysis (can't move arm or leg) or death by paralyzing the muscles that help people breathe.
ROTAVIRUS	Rotavirus can cause diarrhea which can lead to dehydration and other problems in children.
RUBELLA	Rubella virus can cause rash, mild fever, and arthritis (mostly in women). It is also called German Measles.
TETANUS	A bacterial disease which can cause painful tightening of the muscles, usually all over the body, and can lead to "locking" of the jaw so the victim cannot open his mouth or swallow. Tetanus enters the body through cuts or wounds. It is also called Lockjaw.
VARICELLA	Varicella virus can cause a rash, itching, fever, and

Vaccines	Description of Diseases Prevented by Covered Vaccines
(CHICKENPOX)	tiredness, and can lead to severe skin infection, scars, pneumonia, brain damage, or death. It is also called Chickenpox. The chickenpox virus can be spread from person to person through the air, or by contact with fluid from chickenpox blisters.
Meningococcal	A bacterial disease and a leading cause of bacterial meningitis in children 2 through 18 years old in the United States. Also causes blood infections called meningococcemia. The infection most often affects young healthy individuals and can have a mortality rate of 10-15% despite treatment with antibiotics.
Human papillomavirus (HPV)	Most common sexually transmitted virus in the United Sates. More than half of sexually active men and women are infected with HPV at some time in their lives. Most HPV infections

don't cause any symptoms, and go away on their own. But HPV can cause *cervical cancer* in women, which is the 2nd leading cause of cancer deaths among women around the world. HPV is also associated with several less common cancers, such as vaginal and vulvar cancers in women and other types of cancer in both men and women. It can also cause genital warts and warts in the throat.

In: National Vaccine Injury Compensation ... ISBN: 978-1-63482-528-3
Editor: Preston Torres

Chapter 3

NATIONAL VACCINE INJURY COMPENSATION PROGRAM STATISTICS REPORT*

Health Resources and Services Administration

PETITIONS FILED

Fiscal Year	Total
FY 1988	24
FY 1989	148
FY 1990	1,492
FY 1991	2,718
FY 1992	189
FY 1993	140
FY 1994	107
FY 1995	180
FY 1996	84

* This is an edited, reformatted and augmented version of a report issued by the U.S. Department of Health and Human Services, February 2, 2015.

(Continued)

Fiscal Year	Total
FY 1997	104
FY 1998	120
FY 1999	411
FY 2000	164
FY 2001	216
FY 2002	957
FY 2003	2,592
FY 2004	1,214
FY 2005	735
FY 2006	325
FY 2007	410
FY 2008	417
FY 2009	397
FY 2010	448
FY 2011	386
FY 2012	401
FY 2013	503
FY 2014	633
FY 2015	232
Total	15,747

ADJUDICATIONS [1]

Fiscal Year	Compensable	Dismissed	Total
FY 1989	9	12	21
FY 1990	100	33	133
FY 1991	141	447	588
FY 1992	166	487	653
FY 1993	125	588	713

Fiscal Year	Compensable	Dismissed	Total
FY 1994	162	446	608
FY 1995	160	575	735
FY 1996	162	408	570
FY 1997	189	198	387
FY 1998	144	181	325
FY 1999	98	139	237
FY 2000	125	104	229
FY 2001	86	87	173
FY 2002	104	103	207
FY 2003	56	99	155
FY 2004	62	233	295
FY 2005	60	121	181
FY 2006	69	191	260
FY 2007	82	121	203
FY 2008	147	134	281
FY 2009	134	231	365
FY 2010	180	293	473
FY 2011	265	1,370	1,635
FY 2012	261	2,439	2,700
FY 2013	366	627	993
FY 2014	357	167	524
FY 2015	127	33	160
Total	3,937	9,867	13,804

[1]Generally, petitions/claims are not adjudicated in the same fiscal year as filed. On average, it takes 2-3 years to adjudicate a petition/claim after it is filed.

AWARDS PAID[1]

Fiscal Year	Compensated[2]			Dismissed		Interim Fees		Total Outlays
	# of Awards	Petitioners' Award Amount	Attorneys' Fees/ Cost Payments	# of Payments to Attorneys	Attorneys' Fees/Costs Payments	# of Payments to Attorneys	Attorneys' Fees/ Costs Payments	
FY 1989	6	$1,317,654.78	$54,107.14	0	$0.00	0	$0.00	$1,371,761.92
FY 1990	88	$53,252,510.46	$1,379,005.79	4	$57,699.48	0	$0.00	$54,689,215.73
FY 1991	114	$95,980,493.16	$2,364,758.91	30	$496,809.21	0	$0.00	$98,842,061.28
FY 1992	130	$94,538,071.30	$3,001,927.97	118	$1,212,677.14	0	$0.00	$98,752,676.41
FY 1993	162	$119,693,267.87	$3,262,453.06	272	$2,447,273.05	0	$0.00	$125,402,993.98
FY 1994	158	$98,151,900.08	$3,571,179.67	335	$3,166,527.38	0	$0.00	$104,889,607.13
FY 1995	169	$104,085,265.72	$3,652,770.57	221	$2,276,136.32	0	$0.00	$110,014,172.61
FY 1996	163	$100,425,325.22	$3,096,231.96	216	$2,364,122.71	0	$0.00	$105,885,679.89
FY 1997	179	$113,620,171.68	$3,898,284.77	142	$1,879,418.14	0	$0.00	$119,397,874.59
FY 1998	165	$127,546,009.19	$4,002,278.55	121	$1,936,065.50	0	$0.00	$133,484,353.24
FY 1999	96	$95,917,680.51	$2,799,910.85	117	$2,306,957.40	0	$0.00	$101,024,548.76
FY 2000	136	$125,945,195.64	$4,112,369.02	80	$1,724,451.08	0	$0.00	$131,782,015.74
FY 2001	97	$105,878,632.57	$3,373,865.88	57	$2,066,224.67	0	$0.00	$111,318,723.12
FY 2002	80	$59,799,604.39	$2,653,598.89	50	$656,244.79	0	$0.00	$63,109,448.07
FY 2003	65	$82,816,240.07	$3,147,755.12	69	$1,545,654.87	0	$0.00	$87,509,650.06
FY 2004	57	$61,933,764.20	$3,079,328.55	69	$1,198,615.96	0	$0.00	$66,211,708.71
FY 2005	64	$55,065,797.01	$2,694,664.03	71	$1,790,587.29	0	$0.00	$59,551,048.33
FY 2006	68	$48,746,162.74	$2,441,199.02	54	$1,353,632.61	0	$0.00	$52,540,994.37
FY 2007	82	$91,449,433.89	$4,034,154.37	61	$1,692,020.25	0	$0.00	$97,175,608.51
FY 2008	141	$75,716,552.06	$5,191,770.83	73	$2,511,313.26	2	$117,265.31	$83,536,901.46

Fiscal Year	Compensated [2]			Dismissed		Interim Fees		Total Outlays
	# of Awards	Petitioners' Award Amount	Attorneys' Fees/ Cost Payments	# of Payments to Attorneys	Attorneys' Fees/Costs Payments	# of Payments to Attorneys	Attorneys' Fees/ Costs Payments	
FY 2009	131	$74,142,490.58	$5,404,711.98	36	$1,557,139.53	28	$4,241,362.55	$85,345,704.64
FY 2010	173	$179,387,341.30	$5,961,744.40	56	$1,886,239.95	22	$1,978,803.88	$189,214,129.53
FY 2011	251	$216,319,428.47	$9,572,042.87	403	$5,589,417.19	28	$2,001,770.91	$233,482,659.44
FY 2012	249	$163,491,998.82	$9,104,488.60	1,017	$8,621,182.32	37	$5,420,257.99	$186,637,927.73
FY 2013	375	$254,666,326.70	$13,333,179.53	703	$6,970,278.84	50	$1,454,851.74	$276,424,636.81
FY 2014	365	$202,084,196.12	$11,973,575.82	505	$6,801,345.79	38	$2,493,460.73	$223,352,578.46
FY 2015	177	$83,067,135.53	$4,474,812.40	45	$1,245,066.01	19	$1,044,486.97	$89,831,500.91
Total	3941	$2,885,038,650.06	$121,636,170.55	4925	$65,353,100.74	224	$18,752,260.08	$3,090,780,181.43

[1] "Compensated" are claims that have been paid as a result of a settlement between parties or a decision made by the U.S. Court of Federal Claims (Court). The # of awards is the number of petitioner awards paid, including the attorneys' fees/costs payments, if made during a fiscal year. However, petitioners' awards and attorneys' fees/costs are not necessarily paid in the same fiscal year as when the petitions/claims are determined compensable. "Dismissed" includes the the # of payments to attorneys and the total amount of payments for attorneys' fees/costs per fiscal year. The VICP will pay attorneys' fees/costs related to the claim, whether or not the petition/claim is awarded compensation by the Court, if certain minimal requirements are met. "Total Outlays" are the total amount of funds expended for compensation and attorneys' fees/costs from the Vaccine Injury Compensation Trust Fund by fiscal year.

[2] Due to the populations receiving vaccines added to the VICP in recent years, the proportion of adults to children seeking compensation has changed. Since influenza vaccines (vaccines administered to large numbers of adults each year) were added to the VICP in 2005, many adult claims related to that vaccine have been filed.

CLAIMS FILED AND COMPENSATED OR DISMISSED BY VACCINE [1] FEBRUARY 2015 VACCINES LISTED IN CLAIMS AS REPORTED BY PETITIONERS

Vaccine(s)	Filed			Compensated	Dismissed
	Injury	Death	Total		
DT	69	9	78	24	51
DTaP	374	80	454	179	203
DTaP-Hep B-IPV	62	24	86	30	34
DTaP-HIB	10	1	11	4	3
DTaP-IPV-HIB	24	16	40	6	11
DTP	3,286	696	3,982	1,270	2,706
DTP-HIB	20	8	28	4	21
Hep A-Hep B	18	0	18	9	2
Hep B-HIB	8	0	8	4	3
Hepatitis A (Hep A)	65	5	70	27	20
Hepatitis B (Hep B)	618	54	672	241	363
HIB	25	3	28	12	14
HPV	255	12	267	73	85
Influenza	1,704	84	1,788	985	155
IPV	264	14	278	8	267
Measles	143	19	162	55	107
Meningococcal	40	2	42	27	4
MMR	890	57	947	367	502
MMR-Varicella	30	1	31	15	8
MR	15	0	15	6	9

Vaccine(s)	Filed			Compensated	Dismissed
	Injury	Death	Total		
Mumps	10	0	10	1	9
Nonqualified	85	9	94	1	87
OPV	280	28	308	158	150
Pertussis	4	3	7	2	5
Pneumococcal Conjugate	41	5	46	10	26
Rotavirus	65	1	66	39	17
Rubella	190	4	194	70	123
Td	183	3	186	106	64
Tdap	227	1	228	106	12
Tetanus	97	2	99	43	37
Unspecified	5,411	8	5,419	4	4,749
Varicella	78	7	85	51	20
Grand Total	*14,591*	*1,156*	*15,747*	*3,937*	*9,867*

[1] The number of claims filed by vaccine as reported by petitioners in claims since the VICP began on October 1, 1988, and how many of those have been compensated or dismissed by the U.S. Court of Federal Claims (Court). Claims can be compensated by a settlement between parties or a decision by the Court.

[2] Claims filed for vaccines which are not covered under the VICP.

[3] Insufficient information submitted to make a determination.

This information reflects the current thinking of the United States Department of Health and Human Services on the topics addressed. This information is not legal advice and does not create or confer any rights for or on any person and does not operate to bind the Department or the public. The ultimate decision about the scope of the statutes authorizing the VICP is within the authority of the United States Court of Federal Claims, which is responsible for resolving claims for compensation under the VICP.

National Vaccine Injury Compensation Program (VICP) Adjudication Categories by Vaccine for Claims Filed Calendar Year 2006 to Present[1]

Vaccine Alleged by Petitioner[2]	No. of Doses Distributed US CY 2006 - CY 2013 (Source: CDC)[3]	Compensable			Com-pen-sable Total	Dismissed/ Non-Compen-sable Total	Grand Total
		Conces-sion	Court Decision	Settle-ment			
DT	652,327	1		3	4	4	8
DTaP	75,888,233	12	19	75	106	78	184
DTaP-Hep B-IPV	43,929,797	4	7	18	29	38	67
DTaP-HIB	1,135,474				0	1	1
DTaP-IPV-HIB	39,590,896			6	6	11	17
DTP	0[4]		1	2	3	2	5
DTP-HIB	0[4]				0	1	1
Hep A-Hep B	11,662,755			9	9	2	11
Hep B-HIB	4,796,583	1	1	1	3	1	4
Hepatitis A (Hep A)	124,212,280	6	3	22	31	20	51
Hepatitis B (Hep B)	129,820,136	2	10	40	52	38	90
HIB	83,517,849		1	4	5	4	9
HPV	67,250,524	10	1	65	73	85	158
Influenza[5]	944,000,000	73	81	848	1,002	177	1,179
IPV	58,019,052			4	4	2	6
Measles	135,660			1	1		1
Meningo-coccal	58,412,363	1	2	24	27	4	31
MMR	73,441,556	17	14	56	87	74	161
MMR-Varicella	11,028,270	8		8	16	8	24
Nonqualified[6]	N/A			1	1	22	23
OPV	0	1			1	3	4
Pneumo-coccal Conjugate	132,932,107		1	5	6	13	19

Vaccine Alleged by Petitioner[2]	No. of Doses Distributed US CY 2006 - CY 2013 (Source: CDC)[3]	Compensable			Com-pen-sable Total	Dismissed/ Non-Compen-sable Total	Grand Total
		Conces-sion	Court Decision	Settle-ment			
Rotavirus	70,719,103	3	3	15	21	6	27
Rubella	422,548		1		1		1
Td	55,742,830	5	6	50	61	16	77
Tdap	155,106,848	19	7	87	113	14	127
TETANUS	3,836,052	3		18	21	11	32
Unspecified7	N/A	1		2	3	549	552
Varicella	90,425,492	3	6	23	32	10	42
Grand Total	2,236,678,735	170	164	1,387	1,721	1,194	2,915

DEFINITIONS:

- Compensable – The injured person who filed a claim was paid money by the VICP. Compensation can be achieved through a concession by the Department of Health and Human Services (HHS), a decision on the merits of the claim by a special master or a judge of the United States Court of Federal Claims (Court), or a settlement between the parties.
- Concession: HHS concludes that a petition should be compensated based on a thorough review and analysis of the evidence, including medical records and the scientific and medical literature. The HHS review concludes that the petitioner is entitled to compensation, including a determination either that it is more likely than not that the vaccine caused the injury or the evidence supports fulfillment of the criteria of the Vaccine Injury Table. The Court also determines that the petition should be compensated.
- Court Decision: A special master or the court, within the United States Court of Federal Claims, issues a legal decision after weighing the evidence presented by both sides. HHS abides by the ultimate Court decision even if it maintains its position that the petitioner was not entitled to compensation (e.g., that the injury was not caused by the vaccine).
    - For injury claims, compensable court decisions are based in part on one of the following determinations by the court:
    - The evidence is legally sufficient to show that the vaccine more likely than not caused (or significantly aggravated) the injury; or
    - The injury is listed on, and meets all of the requirements of, the Vaccine Injury Table, and HHS has not proven that a factor unrelated to the vaccine more likely than not caused or significantly aggravated the injury. An injury listed on the Table and meeting all Table requirements is given the legal presumption of causation. It should be noted that conditions are placed on the Table for both scientific and policy reasons.

- Settlement: The petition is resolved via a negotiated settlement between the parties. This settlement is not an admission by the United States or the Secretary of Health and Human Services that the vaccine caused the petitioner's alleged injuries, and, in settled cases, the Court does not determine that the vaccine caused the injury. A settlement therefore cannot be characterized as a decision by HHS or by the Court that the vaccine caused an injury. Claims may be resolved by settlement for many reasons, including consideration of prior court decisions; a recognition by both parties that there is a risk of loss in proceeding to a decision by the Court making the certainty of settlement more desirable; a desire by both parties to minimize the time and expense associated with litigating a case to conclusion; and a desire by both parties to resolve a case quickly and efficiently.
- Non-compensable/Dismissed – The injured person who filed a claim was ultimately not paid money.
  - Non-compensable Court decisions include the following:
    - The Court determines that the person who filed the claim did not demonstrate that the injury was caused (or significantly aggravated) by a covered vaccine or meet the requirements of the Table (for injuries listed on the Table).
    - The claim was dismissed for not meeting other statutory requirements (such as not meeting the filing deadline, not receiving a covered vaccine, and not meeting the statute's severity requirement).
    - The injured person voluntarily withdrew his or her claim.

[1] The date range for this table was selected to reflect the status of the current Program since the inclusion of influenza in July 2005, which now constitutes the majority of all VICP claims.

[2] This is the first vaccine listed by the petitioner in the claim, and other vaccines may be alleged or may form the basis of compensation.

[3] Vaccine doses are self-reported distribution data provided by US-licensed vaccine manufacturers. The data provide an estimate of the annual national distribution and do not represent vaccine administration. In order to maintain confidentiality of an individual manufacturer or brand, the data are presented in an aggregate format by vaccine type.

[4] Whole cell pertussis vaccines were not distributed during this time period.

[5] Flu doses are derived from CDC's FluFinder tracking system, which includes data provided to CDC by US-licensed influenza vaccine manufacturers as well as their first line distributors.

[6] Claims filed for vaccines which are not covered under the VICP.

[7] Insufficient information submitted by petitioner to make an initial determination. The concession was for multiple unidentified vaccines that caused abscess formation at the vaccination site(s), and the settlements were for multiple vaccines later identified in the Special Master's Decisions.

In: National Vaccine Injury Compensation ... ISBN: 978-1-63482-528-3
Editor: Preston Torres

Chapter 4

THE NATIONAL CHILDHOOD VACCINE INJURY ACT AND PREEMPTION: AN OVERVIEW OF *BRUESEWITZ V. WYETH*[*]

Vivian S. Chu

SUMMARY

While recent scientific publications have declared that there appears to be no link between immunizations and autism or other serious medical problems, a recent *Journal of Pediatrics* survey of parents with children between the ages of six months and six years old reveals that about 13% of parents used a vaccination plan that varied from the Centers for Disease Control and Prevention-recommended schedule, because of concerns that receiving multiple vaccinations in a short span of time is less safe than delaying certain vaccines. Whether parents follow the government-recommended schedule or an alternative schedule, should their child suffer harm after receiving a vaccination, they must first seek relief through the National Vaccine Injury Compensation Program.

On February 22, 2011, the Supreme Court issued its decision in *Bruesewitz v. Wyeth*, a case involving the scope of the National Childhood Vaccine Injury Act. The Supreme Court considered whether 42 U.S.C. Section 300aa-22(b)(1) of the act precludes all vaccine design defect claims even if the vaccine's side effects were avoidable, or

[*] This is an edited, reformatted and augmented version of Congressional Research Service, Publication No. R41538, dated October 6, 2011.

whether the vaccine manufacturer has to show on a case-by-case basis that the side effects could not have been avoided by some alternatively designed vaccine. Both parties had fundamentally differing interpretations of the statute's text and of Congress's intent behind the National Childhood Vaccine Injury Act. This report provides an overview of the structure of the Vaccine Act and the relevant facts of the *Bruesewitz* case. It then examines the opinions of the lower court and the Supreme Court decision. Lastly, this report analyzes the impact of the decision both in terms of its potential effect on preemption jurisprudence and ongoing vaccine litigation. It also discusses past congressional legislation related to the Vaccine Injury Act.

INTRODUCTION

In October 2010, the Supreme Court heard oral arguments for *Bruesewitz v. Wyeth*,[1] a case which involves the scope of the National Childhood Vaccine Injury Act. The issue before the Court was whether 42 U.S.C. Section 300aa-22(b)(1) of the act precludes all vaccine design defect claims even if the vaccine's side effects were avoidable,[2] in other words whether the section preempts vaccine design defect claims categorically, or whether the vaccine manufacturer has to show on a case-by-case basis that the side effects could not have been avoided by some alternatively designed vaccine.[3] On February 22, 2011, the Supreme Court issued its decision in *Bruesewitz*, affirming, by a vote of 6-2,[4] the decision of the U.S. Court of Appeals for the Third Circuit that the federal law preempts all design-defect claims against vaccine manufacturers brought by plaintiffs seeking compensation for injury or death caused by the vaccine's side effects.[5]

This report provides an overview of the structure of the Vaccine Act and the relevant facts of the *Bruesewitz* case. It then examines the lower court decisions before reviewing the Supreme Court decision. Finally, it discusses the decision's potential effect on preemption jurisprudence as well as on the existing Vaccine Act litigation.

BACKGROUND OF BRUESEWITZ V. WYETH

The National Childhood Vaccine Injury Act (Vaccine Act) was enacted in 1986[6] and established a national vaccine program to "achieve optimal prevention of human infectious diseases through immunization and ... against adverse reaction to vaccines."[7] Under the Vaccine Act, the National Vaccine Injury Compensation Program (Compensation Program) was established to handle claims against drug manufacturers for vaccine-related injuries and deaths.[8] The Compensation Program has two parts. Part A creates a mandatory forum for the administration of claims by requiring individuals who seek compensation, including the injured party's legal representative, to file a petition in the United States Court of Federal Claims (Vaccine Court).[9] A petitioner is entitled to recover if the affected person (1) received a vaccine covered by the Vaccine Act; (2) suffered a "covered" injury;[10] and (3) it cannot be shown by a preponderance of the evidence that the injuries or death were not caused by the vaccine.[11]

42 U.S.C. Section 300aa-22 (§22) provides:

(a) General Rule. Except as provided in subsections (b), (c), and (e) State law shall apply to a civil action brought for damages for vaccine-related injury or death.

(b) Unavoidable adverse side effects; warnings

(1) No vaccine manufacturer shall be liable in a civil action for damages arising from a vaccine-related injury or death associated with the administration of a vaccine after October 1, 1988, *if the injury or death resulted from side effects that were unavoidable even though the vaccine was properly prepared and was accompanied by proper directions and warnings*. (emphasis added)

(2) For purposes of paragraph (1), a vaccine shall be presumed to be accompanied by proper directions and warnings if the vaccine manufacturer shows that it complied in all material respects with all requirements under the Federal Food, Drug, and Cosmetic Act [21 U.S.C. §§ 301 et seq] and section 262 of this title (including regulations issued under such provisions) applicable to the vaccine and related to vaccine-related injury or death for which the civil action was brought unless the plaintiff shows—

(A) that the manufacturer engaged in the conduct set forth in subparagraph (A) or (B) of section 300aa23(d)(2) of this title, or

(B) by clear and convincing evidence that the manufacturer failed to exercise due care notwithstanding its compliance with such Act and section (and regulations issued under such provisions).

(c) Direct Warnings. No vaccine manufacturer shall be liable for civil action for damages arising from a vaccine-related injury or death associated with the administration of a vaccine after October 1, 1988, solely due to the manufacturer's failure to provide direct warnings to the injured party (or the injured party's legal representative) of the potential dangers resulting from the administration of the vaccine manufactured by the manufacturer.

(d) Construction.—[omitted]

(e) Preemption. No State may establish or enforce a law which prohibits an individual from bringing a civil action against a vaccine manufacturer for damages for a vaccine-related injury or death if such civil action is not barred by this part.

A petitioner who suffers an off-Table, or non-covered, injury may still recover compensation by proving affirmatively that the vaccine caused the injury.[12] Part B permits a petitioner to decline the result of the Vaccine Court and pursue a civil suit in state or federal district court only after a final judgment is issued by the Vaccine Court.[13] Any subsequent civil action is governed by state law, including the applicable statute of limitations, which is stayed pending the outcome of the suit filed in the Vaccine Court.[14] However, Section 300aa-22 places limitations on subsequent civil actions, and it is this section that is at issue in *Bruesewitz v. Wyeth*.

In this case, the plaintiffs/petitioners were the parents of Hannah Bruesewitz. They filed a claim with the Vaccine Court in April 1995, seeking compensation on behalf of their daughter, who suffered from several seizures shortly after receiving the third of five recommended doses of the diphtheria-pertussis-tetanus (DPT) vaccine on April 1, 1992.[15] Hannah was subsequently diagnosed as having residual seizure disorder and developmental delay, for which she will likely require medical care for the remainder of her life. The DPT vaccine that Hannah received was marketed by Wyeth (and its predecessors) under the trade name TRI-IMMUNOL and approved in 1948.[16] TRI-IMMUNOL contained whole, inactivated pertussis cells ("whole-cell") that effectively reduced pertussis infections and associated deaths, but it was linked to a variety of adverse events. In December 1991, the FDA approved Wyeth's application for an alternative DPT vaccine, known as ACEL-IMUNE. ACEL-IMUNE does not contain the "whole-cell" component, and is reportedly less likely to cause adverse events.[17] The FDA initially approved Wyeth's ACEL-IMUNE for use in the fourth and fifth doses of the DPT vaccine, but did not approve its use in the first three doses of the DPT vaccine until December 1996.[18] Thus, for her third dose Hannah received the TRI-

IMMUNOL vaccine because there were no non-whole-cell vaccines commercially available at the time. Wyeth, the defendant/respondent, voluntarily discontinued manufacturing TRI-IMMUNOL in 1998.

Although the plaintiffs filed their complaint with the Vaccine Court, alleging that Hannah suffered covered injuries, the Vaccine Court held a hearing in July 2002 and concluded in December 2002 that Hannah's injuries were off-Table injuries and that the petitioners had not proved causation in fact.[19] On February 14, 2003, the plaintiffs did not accept the Vaccine Court's judgment to dismiss the claim with prejudice, and subsequently brought suit in the Philadelphia County Court of Common Pleas in October 2005.[20] Wyeth removed the action on the basis of diversity jurisdiction to the United States District Court for the Eastern District of Pennsylvania.

United States District Court and Court of Appeals Decisions

In federal district court, the plaintiffs sued for damages to Hannah Bruesewitz, costs, punitive damages, and other legal equitable relief. They alleged four counts against Wyeth:

- Count I alleged that Wyeth *negligently failed to produce* a safer vaccine despite knowledge of the existence and feasibility of such safer alternatives;
- Count II alleged that Wyeth *negligently failed to warn* of the actual dangers associated with the particular batch of DPT vaccine administered to Hannah;
- Count III asserted *strict liability for design defect*, in the existence or feasibility of safer alternative designs for the vaccine rendered the vaccine administered to Hannah defective and unreasonably dangerous; and
- Count IV asserted *strict liability for manufacturing defect*, in that, in addition to the unreasonable danger due to the alleged design defect, the particular dose of vaccine administered to Hannah contained a manufacturing defect that made it "extra-hazardous."[21]

The district court granted Wyeth's motion for summary judgment,[22] concluding that Counts I and III (design defect claims) were preempted by the Vaccine Act and that the plaintiffs failed to raise any genuine issue of material fact as to Counts II and IV (failure to warn and manufacturing defect claims, respectively). The United States Court of Appeals for the Third Circuit (Third Circuit) affirmed the federal district court's decision. On appeal, the Third Circuit addressed three questions presented by the Bruesewitzes: (1) whether Section 22(b)(1) acts as a complete bar to design defect claims; (2) whether the plaintiffs met their burden under Section 22(b)(2) of the Vaccine Act to show that the defendants failed to provide an adequate warning of the alleged dangers of the vaccine; and (3) whether the plaintiffs provided sufficient evidence of a manufacturing defect to survive the defendant's motion for summary judgment.

Design Defect Claims (Counts I + III)

The federal district court agreed with the conclusion and reasoning of three other court decisions that held that the Vaccine Act preempts design defect claims.[23] In holding that the Vaccine Act categorically preempts all design defect claims, it drew four conclusions.[24] First, it held that vaccine manufacturers would not be protected from lawsuits if case-by-case inquiries were permitted. Second, the establishment of a no-fault remedies compensation program suggests that it was Congress's intention to provide manufacturers with immunity, allowing them to improve the safety of their products through the innovation of safer alternative designs.[25] Third, the compensation scheme reflects a balance Congress struck "between the policy of widespread distribution of childhood vaccines and the need to compensate those injured affecting that policy." Lastly, the Vaccine Act preempts state law determinations of whether a vaccine is unavoidably unsafe,[26] because "an FDA-approved vaccine design includes the side-effects of that vaccine, and is therefore, by statutory definition, the unavoidably unsafe product subject to" immunity under the liability principles of the Restatement (Second) of Torts Section 402A comment k.[27]

The Third Circuit upheld the district court's decision, but stated that further analysis was warranted. In particular, the court found Sections 22(a) and (b) to contain express preemption[28] language because, like other provisions in federal law,[29] it "conveys a clear intent to override state law civil action claims in particular, defined circumstances."[30] The court of appeals stated that whether the plaintiffs' claims fell within the scope of preemption "hinge[d] on the word 'unavoidable.'"[31] The plaintiffs argued that it "expressly precludes only those state tort claims involving vaccines with side effects first shown to be 'unavoidable,'" and that "avoidability must first be determined on a case-by-case basis." The defendant, on the other hand, argued that the language "preempts all claims arising from allegations of design defect."[32] The court resolved to look at the language, structure, and legislative history of the act to ascertain the scope of preemption created by Section 22(b), concluding that it could not make such a determination from the statutory text alone.

The Court of Appeals found that the Report from the House Committee on Energy and Commerce (Commerce Report) supported the conclusion that the Vaccine Act preempts all design defect claims.[33] In the court's analysis, most importantly, the Commerce Report "stated in precise and certain terms that its reference to comment k and the language of 22(b) results in immunity for liability for all design defects, whether liability rests on theories of strict liability or negligence" (emphasis in the original).[34] According to the court, any reading of the provision to permit state courts to make case-by-case determinations would exacerbate the "very problems which led to instability in the vaccine market and which caused Congress to intervene."[35] The court acknowledged but did not find reliable a subsequent Report from the House Committee on the Budget (Budget Report) which implicates that whether vaccines are unavoidably unsafe "is [a question] left to the courts to determine in accordance with applicable law."[36] It primarily found "the views of a subsequent Congress [to] form a hazardous basis for inferring the intent of an earlier one"[37] and that without more, it had no grounds to conclude whether the Budget Report was an accurate reflection of what had transpired in committee or of Congress's motivations underlying the enactment of the Vaccine Act in 1986.[38] The Third Circuit concluded that the Commerce Report and other legislative history strongly indicate Congress's intention to preempt the specific claims asserted by the plaintiffs, as it had determined "that DPT manufacturers should be shielded from liability for injuries arising from the whole-cell pertussis vaccine."[39]

Failure-to-Warn Claim (Count II) + Manufacturing Defect (Count IV)

The Court of Appeals affirmed the district court's decision to dismiss the Bruesewitzes' claim that the manufacturer withheld information from doctors about particularly dangerous batches of vaccines. If a failure-to-warn claim is not precluded,[40] the Vaccine Act grants the manufacturer the presumption of a proper warning if the manufacturer shows that it complied with the proper FDA requirements. The plaintiffs then must present evidence that the manufacturer "engaged in fraud or wrongful withholding of information" from the Secretary of Health and Human Services (HHS) either during or after the approval process, or show "by clear and convincing evidence that the manufacturer failed to exercise due care notwithstanding its compliance with [the laws and regulations regarding drug approval proceedings]."[41] In the Bruesewitzes' case, the courts held that Wyeth was entitled to the presumption of proper warning, but concluded that the plaintiffs failed to provide any clear and convincing evidence sufficient for a reasonable jury to find in their favor.[42]

The federal district court also dismissed the plaintiffs' strict liability claim that the particular dose administered to Hannah contained a manufacturing defect that made it "extra-hazardous."[43] While the Vaccine Act did not bar such a claim, the court concluded that none of the evidence offered by the plaintiffs demonstrated that the product was defective or that "the specific lot caused *any* of the adverse reactions, let alone the specific reaction suffered by Hannah."[44] The Third Circuit affirmed the decision of the district court.

THE SUPREME COURT DECISION IN *BRUESEWITZ*

The only issue the Supreme Court agreed to review is whether Section 22(b)(1) precludes all design defect claims or whether a vaccine manufacturer must show on a case-by-case basis that the side effects at issue could not have been avoided by some differently designed vaccine. After hearing oral arguments on October 12, 2010, the Supreme Court issued its decision on February 22, 2011, affirming by a vote of 6-2 the Third Circuit's holding that the Vaccine Act expressly preempts all design defect claims against manufacturers.[45]

Justice Scalia, writing for the majority, found that the text of the Vaccine Act supports an interpretation that the provision at issue preempts all design defect claims, and that this textual reading is supported by the structure of the act. Justice Sotomayor, writing a dissenting opinion, concluded the opposite. The opinions addressed several of the points raised during oral arguments, such as the potential for a superfluous interpretation of the provision, the purpose of the Vaccine Act, and the motivation for vaccine manufacturers to keep their products as up-to-date as science and technology permit.

Textual Interpretation

The Court did not perform the same preemption analysis as the Third Circuit; rather, it began by directly focusing on interpreting the text of Section 22(b)(1), which relieves vaccine manufacturers of liability, "if the injury or death resulted from the side-effects that were unavoidable *even though the vaccine was properly prepared and was accompanied by proper directions and warning*"[46] (emphasis added). Noting that products liability law traditionally establishes three grounds for liability—that is, defective manufacture, inadequate directions or warnings, or defective design—the Court stated that if all three grounds for liability were intended to be preserved, "it would be strange to mention specifically only two, and leave the third to implication."[47] The Court concluded that the provision itself "suggests that the *design* of the vaccine is a given, not subject to question in the tort action"[48] (emphasis in the original). In the Court's reading, the "even though" clause "delineates the preventative measures that a vaccine manufacturer must have taken for a side-effect to be considered 'unavoidable' under the statute."[49] Further, the clause is "meant to signal the unexpected: unavoidable side effects [which] persist *despite* best manufacturing and labeling practices"[50] (emphasis in the original). Thus, according to the Court, "[p]rovided that there were proper manufacture and warning, any remaining side effects, including those resulting from design defects, are deemed to have been unavoidable."[51] It also observed that the term "unavoidable" would have little meaning if a manufacturer could be liable for failure to use a different design because "[a] side effect of a vaccine could *always* have been avoidable by use of a differently designed vaccine not containing the harmful element."[52]

Although the lower courts acknowledged that Congress intended to incorporate the principle of comment k of the Restatement, which exempts from strict liability "unavoidably unsafe products," and that it supported the conclusion that design defect claims are preempted, the Court in *Bruesewitz* dismissed the connection. Determining the word "unavoidably," as utilized by comment k, to be very different from "unavoidable," as found in Section 22(b)(1), the Court found no reason to believe that Congress was invoking comment k when enacting Section 22(b)(1).[53] Even though its own analysis concentrated on the text and structure of the Vaccine Act, the Court further addressed points made by the dissent, which relied heavily on the legislative history of the act. Among other things, the Court pointed out that the 1986 Commerce Report counsels injured parties who cannot prove a manufacturing or labeling defect to "pursue recompense in the compensation system, not the tort system."[54] While the dissent asserted that the 1987 Budget Report is the proper and authoritative guide to the meaning of Section 22(b)(1),[55] the Court immediately critiqued the dissent for using "post-enactment legislative history," stating that it is "not a legitimate tool of statutory interpretation," and that "[t]hose who voted on the relevant statutory language were not necessarily the same persons who crafted statements in the later [Budget] Report."[56]

Lastly, the Court acknowledged the critique that its interpretation would render part of Section 22(b)(1) superfluous, specifically the words "the injury or death resulted from side effects that were unavoidable even though," because Congress could have more simply stated that liability would be barred "if ... the vaccine was properly prepared and was accompanied by proper directions and warnings."[57] In addition to highlighting that the dissent's interpretation has superfluity problems of its own,[58] the Court noted that the rule against giving a portion of text an interpretation which renders it superfluous only applies "if verbosity ... can be eliminated by giving ... the remainder of the text, a competing interpretation," which the Court declared could not be done in this instance.[59]

Structural Argument

In addition to the text of the provision, the majority found that the structure of the Vaccine Act and of vaccine regulation generally supported its conclusion that Section 22(b)(1) preempts all design defect claims. In general, the majority found that

1) the lack of guidance for design defects in contrast to the extensive regulation of manufacturing and warning labels, two of the grounds for liability mentioned in the Vaccine Act, "strongly suggests that design defects were not mentioned because they are not a basis for liability";[60]
2) the Vaccine Act provides its own means of improving vaccine design, the establishment of the National Vaccine Program, and the possibility of license revocation if the FDA concludes the vaccine is unsafe demonstrate that Section 22(b)(1)'s "silence regarding design-defect liability was not inadvertent";[61] and
3) the Vaccine Act's *quid pro quo* structure—that is, manufacturers fund the act's compensation fund from their sales, in exchange for avoiding costly tort litigation—would have little meaning if manufacturers are still liable for claims of design defect.[62]

The dissent took issue with the majority's structural arguments. Primarily, it disagreed with the majority's assertion that Congress intended to preempt design defect claims because the Vaccine Act, according to the majority, provided its own means of assuring improvements in vaccine design. Rather, the dissent stated: "neither the Act nor any other provision of federal law places a legal *duty* on vaccine manufacturers to improve the design of their vaccines to account for scientific and technological advances."[63] Absent clear statutory language, the dissent did not believe that Congress intended "to eliminate the traditional incentive and deterrence functions served by state tort liability in favor of a federal regulatory scheme providing only carrots and no sticks,"[64] and that the majority's decision leaves a "regulatory vacuum in which no one ... ensures that vaccine manufacturers adequately take account of scientific and technological advancements."[65] To this, the majority responded that the Court has never suggested that it was more likely to find preemption only if the compensation scheme or "the congressional substitute operated like the tort system."[66]

Analysis of the *Bruesewitz* Decision

Prior to the decision, supporters of the respondent Wyeth, including the American Academy of Pediatrics, American Medical Association, and Infectious Diseases Society of America, argued that a decision in favor of the Bruesewitzes would leave vaccine manufacturers vulnerable to numerous lawsuits, and "could drive vaccine manufacturers from the market and halt future production and development of childhood vaccines in this country."[67] In contrast, supporters of the Bruesewitzes, such as the National Vaccine Information Center and the Vaccine Injured Petitioners Bar Association, have argued that the approximate 5,000 claimants in Vaccine Court who claim that there is a relationship between autism and the mumps, measles, and rubella (MMR) vaccine and/or other thimerosal-containing vaccines would have no recourse if the Court decided in favor of Wyeth.[68] They further argued that the "practical effect of the Third Circuit's opinion ... [was] to deny justice to [the Bruesewitzes and other claimants] in the Vaccine Program whose cases cannot be fully litigated given the restrictions built into the Program."[69] Although Wyeth argued that a decision in its favor would still leave the Bruesewitzes with the ability to pursue failure-to-warn and manufacturing defect claims, supporters for the Bruesewitzes argued that "in practice, manufacturers rely on precedents that all but subsume manufacturing defect claims and failure to warn claims into design defect claims."[70]

The Supreme Court's decision in *Bruesewitz* arguably has a greater practical, rather than jurisprudential, impact as it could have affected either the ability of manufacturers to continue in the vaccine industry or affected the ongoing and future proceedings of individuals seeking compensation under the Vaccine Act. Given the Court's decision in favor of Wyeth, it remains to be seen how this will influence the ongoing claims of individuals asserting a link between autism and MMR and/or thimerosal-containing vaccines, that is, the Omnibus Autism Proceedings.[71] By August 2010, the U.S. Court of Appeals for the Federal Circuit had affirmed the decisions of the U.S. Court of Federal Claims in two test cases.[72] Both test cases were in favor of HHS and specifically examined the issue of causation, as is required by the Vaccine Act for off-Table injuries. Similar decisions were reached with other test cases.[73] With the Omnibus Autism Proceedings concluded,[74] some claimants may have the option of pursuing their claims against the manufacturers in civil court. But they are precluded from asserting a design defect claim under any theory of negligence. The experience of the Bruesewitzes, whose failure-to-warn and manufacturing defect claims were dismissed for lack of evidence, may further foreshadow the difficulties that current claimants could face in bringing successful claims against the vaccine manufacturers. Separately, recent scientific publications, which have declared that there appears to be no link between immunizations and autism or other serious medical problems, may also hinder current and future claimants' ability to prove their claims.[75]

In terms of jurisprudence, it has been observed that "*Bruesewitz* is unlikely to have a broad impact on preemption of common law tort claims given the unique nature of the congressional compensation scheme."[76] Indeed, the Court found preemption in a "hyper-textual analysis," rather than performing a preemption analysis like the Third Circuit, beginning with the traditional presumption against preemption.[77] Similarly, at least one commentator noted that, unlike the prior 2009-2010 Term where the Court's preemption decisions seemed to "duel over the policy arguments that underpin the preemption debate,"[78] the *Bruesewitz* decision and other product liability preemption cases from the 2010-2011 Term demonstrate that the Court "has resigned itself to a narrow, case-by-case approach to the preemption defense."[79] Because of this shift, future questions on whether state tort law claims are preempted "will be resolved not on the basis of broad policy arguments but rather on a case-by-case analysis of specific statutory language, regulatory history, and federal decision-making," and will depend on "which party succeeds in defining the narrative through which a court will view its analysis."[80] On the other hand, others have observed that the decision is consistent with the Court's evolving trend to view tort lawsuits in its preemption decisions as serving a regulatory function (i.e., deterrence or promotion of certain behaviors) rather than a compensatory function (i.e., redressing private wrongs).[81] From this point of view, the conclusion reached in *Bruesewitz* fits neatly with the Court's past preemption decisions. Arguably, the Court in *Cipollone v. Liggett*, 505 U.S. 504 (1992) began to emphasize the regulatory nature that tort lawsuits serve over the parallel regulatory/compensatory effects of tort lawsuits.[82] Under this continued emphasis of the regulatory paradigm, it is not surprising that Justice Scalia in *Bruesewitz* found the "imposition of tort liability" to impede the Vaccine Act's regulatory goals of improving vaccine designs, because such an imposition could drive manufacturers away and threaten the supply of vaccines, "much as state positive enactments might impose unreasonable burdens on manufacturers to the public good."[83]

Lastly, the *Bruesewitz* decision does not address other issues with the Vaccine Act that have been the subject of some academic discussion. These include (1) the lack of a clear evidentiary standard for scrutinizing the admissibility of scientific evidence,[84] and (2) the lack of a clear understanding of the level of proof necessary to show causation.[85] These issues, which pertain to causation, have become more critical because "most claims are in fact for off-[T]able injuries ... [whereas] in the early years of the program ... ninety percent of the cases were covered [injuries]," in which case causation was presumed.[86] These commentators observe that there has been inconsistency in Special Masters' decisions due to a lack of clarity on these particular issues. For example, under the Vaccine Act, Congress charged the U.S. Court of Federal Claims with promulgating "flexible and informal standards of admissibility of evidence," to govern the Vaccine Act litigation, which are known as the Vaccine Rules.[87] As a result, Special Masters enjoy a great deal of discretion to admit and weigh evidence because the Federal Rules of Evidence do not apply. The Vaccine Rules specifically state that Special Masters "will not be bound by common law or statutory rules of evidence."[88] While it has been noted that the admissibility of evidence has become very similar to the tort system in that Special Masters purport to be following the standards set forth in *Daubert v. Merrell Dow Pharmaceuticals*,[89] they have "openly expressed frustration with the lack of uniform standards by which they reach entitlement decisions."[90] The result appears to be "case-by-case jurisprudence that is void of any cohesive explanation of what it takes to prevail within the Vaccine Program."[91] Similarly, the applicable legal standards governing causal proof in off-Table cases arguably "is a story of mixed signals from the Federal Circuit, ranging from only a minimal showing of medical opinion and circumstantial temporal evidence to mirroring the more stringent standards developed in traditional toxic tort cases."[92] While the *Bruesewitz* decision provides a definitive understanding that design defect claims are precluded from being brought in state court, a lack of resolution on these causation issues may give continued rise to inconsistent case law, thereby creating unpredictability in Vaccine Act litigation for both claimants and vaccine manufacturers.

CONGRESSIONAL LEGISLATION

No legislation has been introduced on this issue in the 112th Congress, though some measures were introduced in the 111th Congress. These and other similar bills have been introduced repeatedly in the past; however, none of them would have directly affected the outcome of the *Bruesewitz* case, nor overturned the Court's decision. In the 111th Congress, these bills were (1) H.R. 2459, the National Vaccine Injury Compensation Program Improvement Act of 2009, by Representative Dan Burton, and (2) H.R. 4096, the National Vaccine Injury Compensation Program Modernization Act of 2009, by Representative Tom Perriello. Both bills would have amended the statute of limitations for filing a petition with the Vaccine Court. Specifically, these bills would have extended the period for filing a petition with the Vaccine Court to within two years after the date of the bill's enactment if an injury or death occurs as a result "of a vaccine set forth in the Vaccine Injury Table that is administered after September 30, 1988, and before the date of the [bill's] enactment."[93] The bills would have also allowed petitions to be filed notwithstanding a previous dismissal for an untimely filing. H.R. 2459 would have also addressed the basis for calculating projected lost earnings, the increase of award in the case of a vaccine-related death, allowing compensation for family counseling expenses as well as interim attorneys' fees.

Congress has conducted oversight hearings on the Compensation Program, among concerns that the program was not meeting its original goals of providing expeditious and fair compensation to individuals who may have suffered harm from vaccinations.[94] The practical effect the *Bruesewitz* decision may have on the autism proceedings could renew Congress's interest in evaluating the Compensation Program. If Congress finds that it wishes to give claimants, such as the 5,000 claimants mentioned above, the ability to pursue design defect claims in state courts, then it may choose to revisit the specific language at issue to clarify if the Vaccine Act precludes design defect claims. In the past, Congress has introduced legislation to overturn a decision by the Supreme Court. One prominent decision was *Riegel v. Medtronic*, where the Court held that the Medical Device Amendments of 1976 (MDA) expressly preempted state tort law claims.[95] In the aftermath, legislation was introduced, though not enacted, that would have amended the MDA to provide "[n]othing in this section shall be construed to modify or otherwise affect any action for damages or the liability of any person under the law of the State."[96] Furthermore, Congress could choose to amend the act to clarify the level of causation needed to be shown in order to provide more stability to the system.

End Notes

[1] Bruesewitz v. Wyeth, 561 F.3d 233 (3d Cir. 2009), *cert. granted*, 559 U.S. __ (2010); 2010 U.S. LEXIS 2266 (U.S. March 8, 2010) (No. 09-152).

[2] Brief for Petitioner at i, Bruesewitz v. Wyeth, No. 09-152 (May 24, 2010).

[3] Brief for Respondent at i, Bruesewitz v. Wyeth, No. 09-152 (July 23, 2010).

[4] Justice Elena Kagan recused herself from this hearing. Robert Barnes, "Justices Split on Childhood-Vaccine Case," Wash. Post, October 13, 2010, at A2.

[5] Bruesewitz v. Wyeth, 562 U.S. ___ ; 131 S. Ct. 1068 (2011).

[6] P.L. 99-660; 100 State 3743, 3756-84 (1986), *codified at* 42 U.S.C. §§300aa-1 *et seq.*

[7] 42 U.S.C. §300aa-1.

[8] 42 U.S.C. §§300aa-10 *et seq.*

[9] *Id.* at §300aa-12.

[10] The Vaccine Act created the "Vaccine Injury Table," which sets forth the "vaccines, the injuries, disabilities, illnesses, conditions, and deaths resulting from the administration" of vaccines for which individuals may seek compensation. *Id.* at §300aa-14. For a complete list of covered vaccines and injuries, *see* Department of Health and Human Services, Human Resources and Services Administration, http://www.hrsa.gov/vaccinecompensation /table.*htm.*

[11] *Id.* at §§300aa-11, 300aa-13.

[12] *See* Grant v. Sec'y of HHS, 956 F.2d 1144, 1148 (Fed. Cir. 1992).

[13] 42 U.S.C. §300aa-21. Upon issuance of a Special Master's decision, each party has 30 days to file a motion to have the United States Court of Federal Claims review the decision. If there is no such motion, the clerk of the United States Court of Federal Claims shall immediately enter a judgment in accordance with the Special Master's decision. The parties may further obtain review of the judgment in the United States Court of Appeals for the Federal Circuit. *Id.* at §§300aa-12(e)-(f). Once judgment has been entered by the United States Court of Federal Claims or by the Court of Appeals for the Federal Circuit, a petitioner may give notice to the court that it will file a civil action in a state or federal district court. *Id.* at §300aa-21(a).

[14] *Id.* at §§300aa-22(a), 21(c), 16(c). For description of typical litigation life cycle of a vaccine-related suit, *see* Miles E. Coleman, *An Overview of the National Childhood Vaccine Injury Act*, 21 S. Carolina Lawyer 41 (May 2010).

[15] Pertussis is the disease also commonly known as whooping cough.

[16] The National Health Institute first issued a product license for TRI-IMMUNOL in 1948 to American Cyanamid Company (Cyanamid). Lederle Laboratories, an unincorporated division of Cyanamid, produced TRI-IMMUNOL. In 1994, American Home Products Corporation (AHPC) acquired Cyanamid, but later changed its name to Wyeth in March 2002.

[17] Brief for Petitioner at 17-19, Bruesewitz v. Wyeth, No. 09-152 (May 24, 2010); *but see* Brief for Respondent at 18- 20, Bruesewitz v. Wyeth, No. 09-152 (July 23, 2010).

[18] The FDA first approved the general acellular pertussis vaccine for use in the first three doses in July 1996 when it approved the license of another pharmaceutical company.

[19] Bruesewitz v. Sec'y of Dep't of HHS, No. 95-0266V, 2002 WL 31965744 at *1 (Fed. Cl. December 20, 2002). Approximately one month before the plaintiffs filed their petition with the Vaccine Court, new regulations that were effective on March 10, 1995, deleted residual seizure disorder as a Table Injury for the DPT vaccine. *Id.* at *17 n.1.

[20] 42 U.S.C. §§300aa-21(a), (c).

[21] Bruesewitz, 508 F. Supp. 2d 430, 435 (E.D. Pa. 2007) [hereinafter Bruesewitz I].

[22] Summary judgment is a preverdict "judgment granted on a claim about which there is no genuine issue of material fact and upon which the movant is entitled to prevail as a matter of law." *Black's Law Dictionary* 1449 (7th ed. 1999).

[23] *See* Blackmon v. American Home Products Corp., 328 F. Supp. 2d 659 (S.D. Tex. 2004); Sykes v. GlaxoSmithKline, 484 F. Supp. 2d 290 (E.D. Pa. 2007); Milantrano v. Lederle Labs, 801 N.Y.S.2d 506 (N.Y. App. Div. 2006). In each of these cases, the plaintiffs had asserted that the vaccine was defectively designed.

[24] The district court's conclusions relied upon the four basic conclusions of the district court in *Sykes v. GlaxoSmithKline*. In *Sykes*, the court found: (1) the purpose of the Vaccine Act to protect vaccine manufacturers from the expense of the tort system would be thwarted by allowing juries to evaluate whether a vaccine was unavoidably unsafe on a case-by-case basis; (2) Congress delegated to the Department of Health and Human Services, rather than the jury system, the role of assuring improvements in the quality, effectiveness, and safety of vaccines; (3) the Vaccine Act protects manufacturers from design defect claims in particular; and (4) comment k of §402A of the Restatement (Second) of Torts supports the understanding that the liability of vaccine manufacturers is limited to claims that the vaccine deviated from its FDA-approved design. Sykes, 484 F. Supp. 2d at 301-03.

[25] Bruesewitz I, 508 F. Supp. 2d at 445.

[26] *Id.* at 445-46.

[27] *Id.* at 446. Restatement (Second) of Torts §402A cmt. k (1965) states:

Unavoidable unsafe products. There are some products which, in the present state of human knowledge, are quite incapable of being made safe for their intended and ordinary use.... An outstanding example is the vaccine for the Pasteur treatment of rabies, which not uncommonly leads to very serious and damaging consequences when it is injected.... Such a product, properly prepared, and accompanied by proper directions and warning, is not defective, nor is it *unreasonably* dangerous.... The seller of such products, again with the qualification that they are properly prepared and marketed, and proper warning is given, where the situation calls for it, is not to be held to strict liability for unfortunate consequences attending their use, merely because he has undertaken to supply the public with an apparently useful and desirable product, attended with a known but apparently reasonable risk.

The court in *Blackmon* acknowledged that comment k of the Restatement only applies to strict liability. However, it concluded that §22(b)(1) would preclude a design defect claim under all theories of liability because the section grants immunity in a "civil action for damages." Blackmon, 328 F. Supp. 2d at 665.

[28] Bruesewitz v. Wyeth, 561 F. 3d 233, 240-41 (3d Cir. 2009) [hereinafter Bruesewitz II]. Generally there are three types of preemption: express, implied, or field preemption. Express preemption exists where a federal law contains explicit language of Congress's intention to preempt state law. In such cases, courts are often called upon to "identify the domain expressly pre-empted by that language." Medtronic, Inc v. Lohr, 518 U.S. 470 484 (1996) (internal quotation marks and citations omitted). Implied preemption arises when state law conflicts with a federal statute when it is "impossible for a private party to comply with both state and federal requirements," English v. General Electric, Co., 496 U.S. 72, 78-9 (1990), or when state law "stands as an obstacle to the accomplishment and execution of the full purpose and objectives of Congress." Hines v. Davidowitz, 312 U.S. 52, 67 (1941). Field preemption arises when state law occupies a "field reserved for federal regulation." United States v. Locke, 529 U.S. 89, 111 (2000). With respect to design defect claims, the court of appeals found that the district court's decision was consistent with an express preemption analysis and rejected the plaintiffs' claim that the district court's decision was based on implied or field preemption grounds. Bruesewitz II, 561 F.3d at 251.

[29] For example, the court found the language of §22(b)—"[n]o vaccine manufacturer shall ..."—to be similar to the Federal Cigarette Labeling and Advertising Act's "No statement relating to smoking and health other than the statement required by section 1333 of this title, shall be required on any cigarette package." 15 U.S.C. §1334. The Supreme Court in *Lorillard Tobacco Co. v. Reilly*, 533 U.S. 525 (2001) had construed this provision as express preemption provisions.

[30] Bruesewitz II, 561 F.3d at 243.

[31] *Id.* at 245.

[32] *Id.*

[33] H.Rept. 99-908 (1986).

[34] Bruesewitz II, 561 F. 3d at 247-8 (*citing* H.Rept. 99-908 at 25-26) ("If the [injured individuals] cannot demonstrate under applicable law either that a vaccine was improperly prepared or that it was accompanied by improper directions or inadequate warnings [they] should pursue recompense in the compensation system, not the tort system." *Id.* at 26).

[35] *Id.* at 249.

[36] *Id.* (*citing* H.Rept. 100-391, pt. 1 at 691 (1987)). The court found the Budget Report's repeated use of the term "the Committee" problematic because it was unclear whether this referred to the Commerce and Energy Committee from 1986, which had jurisdiction over the Vaccine Act, or the Budget Committee, which played no role in the drafting or passage of the act. *Id.* at 250.

[37] *Id.* at 250 (quotation marks omitted) (*citing* United States v. Price, 361 U.S. 304, 313 (1960)).

[38] *Id.*

[39] *Id.* Both the Commerce Report and a background report issued by the staff of the Energy and Commerce Committee contained numerous references to the DPT vaccine, its development, the side effects, hurdles in clinical testing, and the high number of lawsuits against the only two producers of the vaccine. *Id.* at 251 (*citing* Staff of H. Comm. on Energy & Commerce, 99th Cong., *Childhood Immunizations*, at III (1986)).

[40] Section 22(c) of the Vaccine Act "clearly bars failure-to-warn claims based on a failure to directly warn the injured party's legal representative"; however, the court in *Blackmon*

found that allegations of failure-to-warn "doctors and medical intermediaries" are not subject to the prohibition of §22(c). Bruesewitz I, 508 F. Supp. 2d. at 447 (*citing* Blackmon, 328 F. Supp. 2d at 666).

[41] *Id.* at 447 (*citing* 42 U.S.C. §§300aa-22(b)(2)(A) and (B)).

[42] In support of their failure-to-warn claim, the plaintiffs identified the lot that produced the dose of TRI-IMMUNOL administered to Hannah as well the Vaccine Adverse Event Reporting System report confirming deaths and other adverse events associated with the lot. Lots associated with deaths and adverse reactions are sometimes referred to as "hot lots." However, according to the evidence, a "hot lot" is not defined by the total number of adverse incidents, but rather by the rate at which those incidents occurred. The plaintiffs had produced no evidence from which a trier of fact could infer that the dose in question originated in a lot of vaccine associated with a disproportionate number of adverse health effects. Bruesewitz I, 508 F. Supp. 2d at 448; Bruesewitz II, 561 F.3d at 254-254.

[43] Bruesewitz I, 508 F. Supp. at 435 (*citing* Pl. Am. Comp. ¶ 37). The plaintiffs asserted that the dose administered to Hannah had "an inappropriate balance between neuro-toxins and endo-toxins in the pertussis vaccine." *Id.* Wyeth disputed this allegation by submitting the Declaration of Dr. Mary B. Ritchy, Ph.D, who stated that "The pertussis bacterium does not contain a recognized 'neuro-toxin' component." *Id.* at 449.

[44] *Id.* at 451.

[45] Bruesewitz v. Wyeth, 562 U.S. __ ; 131 S. Ct. 1068 (2011). Chief Justice Roberts and Justices Kennedy, Thomas, Breyer, and Alito joined in Justice Scalia's majority opinion. Justice Sotomayor wrote a dissenting opinion, which Justice Ginsburg joined.

[46] 42 U.S.C. §300aa-22(b)(1).

[47] Bruesewitz, 131 S. Ct. at 1075-1076 (*citing* W. Keeton, d. Dobbs, R. Keeton, & D. Owen, Prosser, and Keeton on Law of Torts 695 (5th ed. 1984)).

[48] *Id.* at 1075.

[49] *Id.*

[50] *Id.* at 1077. Specifically, the Court notes that "even though" is a concessive subordinating conjunction and that the dissent's reading of the "even though" clause treats it as a coordinating junction like "and" that links together independent ideas. *Id.* It disagreed with the dissent's treatment of the word "even though," stating that the dissent's treatment makes preemption "turn equally on unavoidability, proper preparation, and proper labeling." *Id.*

[51] *Id.* 1075.

[52] *Id.* The dissent criticized this assertion by noting that this reading "entirely ignores the fact that removing the 'harmful element' will often result in a less effective or entirely ineffective vaccine." According to the dissent, the legislative history of the Vaccine Act makes clear that a side effect is "unavoidable" only "where there is no feasible alternative design that would eliminate the side effect of the vaccine without compromising its cost and utility." *Id.* at 1094 (dissenting opinion).

[53] *Id.* at 1077 (majority opinion). Notably, the Court stated that comment k "creates a special category of 'unavoidably unsafe products,' while the statute refers to 'side effects that were unavoidable.'" *Id.* The dissent spent much time arguing that the legislative history—the 1986 Commerce Report—demonstrates Congress's intent to codify the principle in comment k, meaning that "unavoidable" is best understood as a term of art that incorporates the commonly understood meaning of "unavoidably unsafe" products. *Id.* at 1088-1091 (dissenting opinion). Furthermore, that many courts in 1986, in applying comment k to the term "unavoidable," interpreted it to require a "case-specific showing that the product was

'quite incapable of being made safer for its intended use,'" did not have any bearing on the Court's conclusion. *Id.* at 1077 (majority opinion).

[54] *Id.* at 1081 (*citing* H.Rept. 99-908 at 26).

[55] *Id.* at 1092 (dissenting opinion). Specifically, the dissent highlighted a passage in the 1987 Budget Report as stating "the codification of Comment (k) ... was not intended to decide as a matter of law the circumstances in which the vaccine should be deemed unavoidably safe." *Id.*

[56] *Id.* at 1081 (majority opinion).

[57] *Id.* at 1078.

[58] The Court stated that the dissent's interpretation renders the passage "even though the vaccine was properly prepared ..." superfluous because it would have been sufficient for Congress to say "if the injury or death resulted from side effects that were unavoidable," if Congress, under the dissent's interpretation, requires a case-by-case determination of avoidable side effects. In response, the dissent stated the "even though" clause establishes two additional prerequisites—proper manufacturing and proper labeling—to qualify for exemption from liability under §22(b)(1). Thus, under the dissent's interpretation a vaccine manufacturer, even if it demonstrated that the side effects were unavoidable, would still have to prove that it properly manufactured and labeled the vaccine. *Id.* at 1091 (dissenting opinion).

[59] *Id.* at 1095 (majority opinion). In other words, because the passage "if the injury or death ... unavoidable" cannot be interpreted to require a case-specific determination of avoidable injuries under the Court's interpretation, the Court is therefore not prevented from reading §22(b)(1) in such a manner that renders the aforementioned phrase superfluous.

[60] *Id.* at 1079.

[61] *Id.* at 1080.

[62] *Id.* at 1079-1080.

[63] *Id.* at 1097 (dissenting opinion).

[64] *Id.* at 1098-1099. In the dissent's view, "the normal competitive forces that spur innovation and improvements to existing product lines in other markets [] operate with less force in the vaccine market, particularly for vaccines that have already been released and marketed to the public." *Id.*

[65] *Id.* at 1101.

[66] *Id.* at 1079 (majority opinion).

[67] Jennifer Couzin-Frankel, "Closely Watched Vaccine Injury Claim Reaches Supreme Court," *Science*Insider October 12, 2010, http://news.sciencemag.org/scienceinsider/2010/10 /closely- watched-vaccine-injury.html.

[68] National Vaccine Injury Compensation Program (NVIC) - About the Omnibus Autism Proceeding, http://www.hrsa.gov/vaccinecompensation/omnibusautism.html. NVIC argued that because the "overwhelming majority of cases in vaccine court today are 'off-table,'" (i.e., not injuries recognized by the Vaccine Injury Table; see note 10) the parties in those situations are "unable to take advantage of presumptive causation" and ultimately would have to participate in costly, time-consuming causation hearings, which are highly adversarial and generally end without compensation. *See* Brief of *Amici Curiae* National Vaccine Information Center, Its Cofounders and 24 Other Organizations In Support of Petitioners at 14, Bruesewitz v. Wyeth, No. 09-152 (May 24, 2010).

[69] Brief of Vaccine Injured Petitioners Bar Association (VIPBA), The George Washington University Law School Vaccine Injury Clinic, and Zenoria Phillips Deloatch of Moshella F. Roberts, as *Amici Curiae* in Support of Petitioners at 24-25, Bruesewitz v. Wyeth, No. 09-

152 (May 24, 2010). They noted that in order for the Vaccine Act to provide "swift and simple justice," Congress put in "[r]estrictions on discovery, evidence, and motion practices ... to speed up the process," but that given these limits, the "Vaccine Program cannot provide satisfactory relief for every family of a vaccine-injured child." *Id.* at 25. Knowing that the tool of discovery in litigation creates incentives for greater vaccine safety, VIPBA emphasized that this "inspired Congress to keep the tort option available as a safety incentive." *Id.* at 21.

[70] *Id.* at 24-25 n.8.

[71] The Omnibus Autism Proceedings were formed to address the approximately 5,000-plus autism claims pending before the Vaccine Court. A panel of attorneys representing various petitioners identified three general theories of causation: (1) that vaccines containing thimerosal, when combined with the MMR vaccine, can cause autism; (2) that vaccines containing thimerosal alone can cause autism; and (3) that the MMR vaccine alone can cause autism. The panel selected three test cases each for each theory of causation asserted, and assigned each test case to a separate Special Master for adjudication. *See* U.S. Court of Federal Claims, Office of Special Masters, *The Autism Proceedings*, http://www.uscfc.uscourts.gov/sites/default/files/autism.background.2010.pdf.

[72] *See* Hazlehurst v. Sec'y of HHS, 605 F.3d 1343 (Fed. Cir. 2010) (affirming decision of lower court to deny the petition, given lack of evidence to prove causation between the MMR vaccine and development of autism); Cedillo v. Sec'y of HHS, 617 F.3d 1328 (Fed. Cir. 2010) (affirming decision of lower court to deny petition, given lack of evidence to prove causation between the MMR vaccine in conjunction with thimerosal-containing vaccines and development of autism).

[73] For theory number two—establishing causation of thimerosal-containing vaccines only—the Special Masters rejected the petitioners' petitions. *See* Mead v. Sec'y of HHS, Decision of Special Master Campbell-Smith, Case No. 03-215V (Mar. 12, 2010); King v. Sec'y of HHS, Decision of Special Master Hastings, Case No. 03-584V (March 12, 2010); and Dwyer v. Sec'y of HHS, Decision of Special Master Vowell, Case No. 03-1202V (March 12, 2010).

[74] *See In Re: Claims for Vaccine Injuries Resulting in Autism Spectrum Disorder or Similar Neurodevelopmental Disorder*, Update January 12, 2011, http://www.uscfc.uscourts.gov/sites/default/files/autism/ Autism%20Update%201%2012%2011.pdf.

[75] Rob Stein, "Vaccines are generally safe, National Academy of Sciences says," *Washington Post* (August 25, 2011); CNN Release, *Retracted autism study an 'elaborate fraud,' British journal finds*, January 5, 2011, http://www.cnn.com/2011/HEALTH/01/05/autism.vaccines/index.html.

[76] Mary J. Davis, *The Case Against Preemption: Vaccines & Uncertainty*, 8 Ind. Health L. Rev. 291, 307 (2011).

[77] Bruesewitz II, 561 F.3d at 240 ("[C]ourts must begin their analysis of these [preemption] questions by applying a presumption against preemption. *Cipollone v. Liggett Group*, 505 U.S. 504 (1992). 'In areas of traditional state regulation, we assume that a federal statute has not supplanted state law unless Congress has made its intention 'clear and manifest.' *Bates v. DowAgroSciences*, 544 U.S. 431 (2005).").

[78] Eric G. Lasker, *U.S. Supreme Court Preemption Trilogy: The Sequel*, Washington Legal Foundation: Legal Backgrounder Vol. 26, No. 7 (March 25, 2011). For example, in *Riegel v. Medtronic*, 522 U.S. 312 (2008) and *Wyeth v. Levine*, 129 S. Ct. 1187 (2009), Justice Scalia emphasized a strong policy argument in support of preemption, namely that "juries are ill-equipped to perform the FDA's cost-benefit-balancing function ... [and] tend to focus

on the risk of a particular products design or warning label [rather than] the overall benefits of that design or label." *See* Wyeth, 129 S. Ct. at 1229-30. On the other side of the debate, Justice Ginsberg in both *Riegel* and *Wyeth* emphasized the policy argument that FDA regulations and state tort liability operate independently, and that state law offers an additional layer of consumer protection that is complementary to FDA regulation. Lasker, at *2.

[79] Lasker observed that Justice Scalia in *Bruesewitz* focused more on a grammatical analysis of the statutory language and less on building upon his earlier policy arguments in support of preemption. Lasker, *supra* note 78, at *3. Likewise, in *Williamson v. Mazda*, 131 S. Ct. 1131 (2011), another preemption case in the 2010-2011 Term, the Court's decision against a finding of implied preemption was based on narrow grounds; that is, implied preemption turned on the significance or insignificance of the policies underlying a particular regulatory decision. Lasker, *supra* note 78, at *4.

[80] Lasker, *supra* note 78, at *4.

[81] Christina Wells, William E. Marcantel, and Dave Winters, *Preemption of Tort Lawsuits: The Regulatory Paradigm in the Roberts Court*, 40 Stetson L. Rev. 793 (2011). Relying on a regulatory paradigm, it is arguably easier for the Court to read express preemption words such as "laws," "requirements," or "standards," as applying to not only state statutes but tort claims as well. *Id.* at 793, 818. For example, in 1992, the Court in *Cipollone v. Liggett Group*, 505 U.S. 504 (1992), focused on the regulatory effect of tort lawsuits when it interpreted the express preemptive provisions in the Public Health Cigarette Smoking Act of 1969 to bar not only conflicting state "laws," "rules," and standards," but state tort lawsuits as well. Similarly, the Court emphasized the regulatory function of state tort lawsuits in *Riegel v. Medtronic*, 522 U.S. 312 (2008), when it found preemption of state tort law claims involving Class III medical devices. However, the Court has also emphasized the regulatory function of tort lawsuits even where it has rejected a preemption argument, finding generally the tort system to be a complementary form of regulation. *See, e.g.*, Wyeth v. Levine, 129 S. Ct. 1187 (2009) (finding that the Federal Food Drug and Cosmetic Act did not preempt a state tort lawsuit based upon the manufacturer's failure-to-warn, in part, because the tort system acts as a "complementary form of drug regulation"); Williamson v. Mazda, 131 S. Ct. 1131 (2011) (finding no preemption of wrongful death claims because such lawsuits do not conflict with the federal regulatory objective of auto safety).

[82] Wells, *supra* note 81, at 807.

[83] Wells, *supra* note 81, at 816. *See also* James M. Beck, *The Food, Drug, and Cosmetic Act: Searching for Crossroads of Safety and Innovation: Federal Preemption in FDA-Regulated Product Liability Litigation*, 32 Hamline L. Rev. 657 (2009) (arguing that the Court's decisions in *Cipollone v. Liggett Group* and *Geier v. Am. Honda Motor Co.* where it found express and implied preemption, respectively, eliminated any "doctrinal impediments" to preemption and cleared the way for FDA-regulated drug and medical device manufacturers to assert that FDA regulation had a preemptive effect).

[84] Brandon Boxler, *What to do with Daubert: How to Bring Standards of Reliable Scientific Evidence to the National Vaccine Injury Compensation Program*, 52 Wm. & Mary L. Rev. 1319 (March 2011).

[85] Betsy J. Grey, *The Plague of Causation in the National Childhood Vaccine Injury Act*, 48 Harv. J. on Legis. 343 (Summer 2011).

[86] Robert L. Rabin, *The Vaccine No-Fault Act: An Overview*, 8 Ind. Health L. Rev. 267 (2011). The drafters of the Compensation Program may not have anticipated this change in

dynamic, that is, the increase of off-Table injury claims compared to covered injury claims, because they intended the Vaccine Injury Table to be the centerpiece of the program. As a result, it is possible that less attention was paid to providing clear guidelines to the Vaccine Court on how to resolve off-Table injury claims. Grey, *supra* note 85, at 346.

[87] 42 U.S.C. §300aa-12(d)(2).

[88] Vaccine R. Fed. Cl. 8(b)(1), *available at* http://www.uscfc.uscourts.gov/sites/default/files/11.07.15finalversionofvaccinerules.pdf.

[89] Rabin, *supra* note 86, at 271.

[90] Boxler, *supra* note 84, at 1340.

[91] *Id.* at 1341. For example, in *Curcuas v. Sec'y of HHS*, 26 Cl. Ct. 537 (1992), the Court of Federal Claims affirmed a Special Master's finding that the DPT vaccine cannot—and-did not—cause chronic encephalopathies because he found an Institute of Medicine Report (IOM) was more persuasive than the conflicting expert testimony of Dr. Mark Geier. In contrast, one year later in *Estep ex rel. Estep v. Sec'y of HHS*, 28 Fed. Cl. 664, 668-69, the Court of Federal Claims affirmed a decision by the same Special Master who had reached a conclusion opposite from *Curcuas*, finding Dr. Geier's testimony to prove more persuasive than the IOM report.

[92] Grey, *supra* note 85, at 379. For example, the Federal Circuit rejected a stringent five-prong test for establishing causation in the off-Table injury claims and "re-imposed on petitioners a three-part evidentiary test: (1) medical theory causally connecting the vaccination and the injury; (2) a logical sequence of cause and effect showing the vaccination was the reason for the injury; and (3) a showing of proximate temporal relationship between vaccine and injury." *Althen v. Sec'y of HHS (Althen III)*, 418 F.3d 1274 (Fed. Cir. 2005). Despite this standard, a recent decision by the Federal Circuit, *Moberly ex rel. Moberly v. Sec'y of HHS*, 592 F.3d 1315 (Fed. Cir. 2010), has suggested that "the relaxed presumptions applicable to Table injuries may not satisfy causal proof for non-Table claims and that traditional tort standards should apply." *Id.* at 1332.

[93] 111th Congress, H.R. 2459, Section 7; H.R. 4096, Section 2 (2009).

[94] *Compensating Vaccine Injuries: Are Reforms Needed? Before Subcomm. On Criminal Justice, Drug Policy, and Human Resources of the H. Comm. On Gov't Reform*, 106th Cong. 1 (1999); *National Vaccine Injury Program: Is It Working As Congress Intended? Before H. Comm. On Gov't Reform*, 107th Cong. 1 (2001); *Continuing Oversight of the National Vaccine Injury Compensation Program Before H. Comm. On Gov't Reform*, 107th Cong. 1 (2002).

[95] 128 S. Ct. 999 (2008). For more information on this case, see CRS Report R40534, *Riegel v. Medtronic, Inc.: Federal Preemption of State Tort Law Regarding Medical Devices with FDA Premarket Approval*, by Vanessa K. Burrows.

[96] 111th Congress, H.R. 1346, Medical Devices Safety Act; S. 540, Medical Devices Safety Act (2009).

INDEX

A

access, 20, 38
Administrative Office of the United States Courts, 27
administrative support, 27
adults, 17, 25, 26, 34, 37, 59
adverse event, 68, 82
affirming, 66, 72, 84
age, 34
agencies, 4, 5, 22, 38
allergic reaction, viii, 39, 47, 48, 49
anaphylactic shock, 28, 29
anaphylaxis, 47
appropriations, 5, 18, 35, 38
Appropriations Committee, 37
arthritis, 28, 52
audit, 5
authority, 6, 61
autism, 10, 11, 13, 14, 36, 65, 75, 76, 78, 84
awareness, 4, 25, 26, 27

B

bacterial infection, 52
bacterium, 82
behaviors, 77
benefits, 9, 21, 22, 85
blood, 48, 51, 53
bones, 51
brain, 48, 51, 52
brain damage, 52
breathing, 51
Budget Committee, 81

C

cancer, 53
cancer death, 53
caregivers, 25
case law, 78
causation, vii, 1, 4, 6, 13, 16, 17, 36, 63, 69, 76, 77, 79, 83, 84, 86
CDC, 62, 64
cervical cancer, 53
chicken, 36
chicken pox, 36
Chief Justice, 82
childhood, 36, 40, 70, 75
children, 6, 8, 15, 17, 24, 26, 29, 31, 34, 35, 36, 37, 52, 53, 59, 65
cirrhosis, 52
citizens, 40
civil action, 67, 68, 70, 79, 81
civil law, 50
clarity, 77
CNN, 84
common law, 76, 77
communication, 25
community(s), 28, 36

compensation, vii, viii, 1, 2, 3, 4, 5, 6, 7, 8, 12, 13, 14, 17, 18, 19, 20, 21, 22, 24, 26, 27, 32, 33, 34, 35, 37, 38, 40, 41, 42, 47, 59, 61, 63, 64, 66, 67, 68, 70, 73, 74, 75, 76, 78, 79, 81, 83
compensatory effect, 77
compliance, 67, 71
confidentiality, 23, 24, 64
conflict, 85
Congress, 3, 16, 38, 40, 66, 70, 71, 73, 74, 77, 78, 80, 81, 82, 83, 84, 86
congressional budget, 5, 35
consensus, 33
consumer protection, 85
cost, 3, 22, 24, 32, 33, 82, 84
cough, 52
coughing, 52
counseling, 78
Court of Appeals, 46, 66, 69, 70, 71, 76, 79
covering, 51, 52
criticism, 26

D

damages, 8, 37, 67, 69, 79, 81
danger, 69
data collection, 5
deaths, vii, 1, 26, 33, 34, 38, 45, 67, 68, 79, 82
defects, 71, 73, 74
defendants, 70
dehydration, 52
Department of Health and Human Services, viii, 2, 3, 39, 40, 55, 61, 63, 79, 80
Department of Justice, viii, 3, 4, 19, 22, 40
Department of the Trcasury, 2, 3, 5
deterrence, 75, 77
diabetes, 36
diarrhea, 51, 52
disability, 29, 33
diseases, 35, 41, 47, 66
disorder, 15, 68, 80
disposition, 8
dissenting opinion, 72, 82, 83
distribution, 64, 70
diversity, 69
doctors, 40, 43, 71, 82
DOJ, vii, viii, 2, 3, 4, 5, 7, 8, 12, 16, 17, 18, 19, 21, 22, 27, 33, 36, 37, 38, 40, 46
draft, 27, 38

E

earnings, 37, 49, 78
EEG, 43, 44
e-mail, 25
emotional distress, 37
encephalitis, 28
environment, 24, 26
equipment, 22
evidence, 2, 5, 6, 7, 8, 12, 16, 34, 36, 63, 67, 70, 71, 72, 76, 77, 82, 84
execution, 81
exercise, 12, 67, 71
expertise, 34

F

faith, 20, 35, 49, 50
family members, 23
FDA, 68, 70, 71, 74, 80, 84, 85, 86
federal agency, 33
federal law, 66, 70, 75, 81
Federal Register, 4
fever, 52
financial, 38
fiscal year 2009, 2, 3, 9, 10, 11, 12, 15, 18, 21, 35
fluid, 52
force, 83
formation, 64
fraud, 71, 84
FTE, 3, 21, 22, 33
full-time equivalent, 3, 21, 22, 33
funding, 38
funds, 4, 6, 22, 59

G

GAO, vii, viii, 1, 2, 6, 10, 11, 14, 19, 20, 21, 22, 29, 32, 33, 34, 37, 38
General Services Administration, 22
genital warts, 53
government securities, 35
grants, 71, 81
greed, 72
grouping, 9, 36
guardian, 42
guidance, 74
guidelines, 86

H

HBV, 40, 47
headache, 52
health, 8, 25, 40, 81, 82
Health and Human Services (HHS), vii, viii, 2, 3, 4, 5, 6, 7, 8, 11, 13, 14, 15, 16, 22, 23, 24, 26, 27, 31, 33, 34, 35, 36, 37, 38, 40, 43, 45, 46, 63, 64, 71, 76, 79, 80, 84, 86
health care, 8, 25
health care professionals, 25
health effects, 82
heart failure, 51
hemophilus influenza, 15, 29
hemophilus influenza type b, 15
hepatitis, 16, 29, 36, 37, 45
history, 71, 73, 76, 82
hospitalization, 43
House, 3, 71
House of Representatives, 3
HPV, 29, 40, 49, 53, 60, 62
human, 16, 29, 37, 66, 80

I

identification, 27
immune response, 48
immune system, 15
immunity, 70, 71, 81
immunization, 66
improvements, 75, 80, 83
income, 3, 5, 18, 19, 37
individuals, vii, 1, 2, 5, 6, 15, 23, 25, 26, 33, 34, 53, 67, 76, 78, 79, 81
industry, 76
infection, 48, 51, 52, 53
influenza, 15, 16, 17, 18, 26, 29, 30, 31, 36, 59, 64
influenza vaccine, 15, 16, 17, 18, 26, 29, 31, 59, 64
injury(s), vii, 1, 2, 3, 4, 5, 6, 7, 8, 10, 12, 14, 15, 16, 17, 18, 23, 24, 26, 29, 31, 33, 34, 36, 37, 38, 41, 42, 44, 45, 46, 47, 48, 49, 50, 63, 64, 66, 67, 68, 69, 71, 72, 74, 76, 77, 78, 79, 83, 86
injury claims, 8, 15, 23, 34, 36, 63, 86
intermediaries, 82
intussusception, 15, 37
investment(s), 3, 18, 19, 35, 37
issues, 4, 6, 7, 23, 25, 33, 34, 63, 77

J

jaundice, 51, 52
joints, 49, 51, 52
judiciary, 34
juries, 80, 84
jurisdiction, 69, 81
justification, 16, 38

L

labeling, 73, 82, 83
laws, vii, 2, 4, 39, 72, 85
laws and regulations, 72
lawyers, 7, 49, 50
lead, 8, 51, 52
legislation, 66, 78, 79
legislative proposals, 38
life cycle, 79
lifetime, vii, 1, 3
litigation, 25, 37, 66, 74, 77, 79, 84
liver, 51, 52

liver cancer, 52
liver damage, 52
liver disease, 51
loss of appetite, 52

M

majority, 10, 20, 26, 64, 72, 74, 82, 83
management, 18
manufacturing, 69, 72, 73, 74, 75, 76, 83
marketing, 25
Maryland, 41, 50
materials, 8
matter, 80, 83
measles, 13, 28, 35, 37, 75
media, 25
medical, vii, 1, 3, 7, 12, 13, 16, 22, 24, 38, 41, 42, 43, 45, 46, 47, 49, 63, 65, 68, 76, 78, 82, 85, 86
medical care, vii, 1, 3, 24, 68
meningitis, 36, 51, 52, 53
meningococcemia, 53
mercury, 13
messages, 25
military, 42
mortality, 53
mortality rate, 53
motivation, 72
MR, 28, 40, 48, 49, 60
mumps, 13, 28, 30, 35, 37, 40, 75
muscles, 52

N

National Academy of Sciences, 84
National Vaccine Injury Compensation Program, 1, iii, v, 2, 3, 10, 11, 14, 19, 20, 21, 22, 29, 31, 32, 35, 37, 38, 39, 50, 55, 62, 65, 67, 78, 83, 85, 86
negotiation, 7
nerve, 49
nervous system, 15
neuritis, 28
neurodevelopmental disorders, 13
nurses, 40, 43

O

obstruction, 15
Office of Management and Budget, 35
officials, vii, 2, 4, 15, 16, 23, 25, 35, 37, 38
outreach, 23, 24, 25, 27, 38
ovaries, 52
oversight, 78

P

pain, 4, 37, 49, 52
parallel, 77
paralysis, 15, 51, 52
parents, 5, 13, 23, 25, 65, 68
participants, 25
permit, 71, 72
personal views, 33
persuasion, 34
pertussis, 28, 37, 40, 47, 64, 68, 71, 80, 82
pharmaceutical, 80
Philadelphia, 69
platelets, 48
pneumonia, 51, 52
policy, 63, 70, 76, 84, 85
polio, 28, 48
polysaccharide, 31, 36
population, 35
precedents, 75
prejudice, 69
preparation, 82
preservative, 13
prevention, 66
principles, 70
private party, 81
producers, 81
public awareness, 24, 38
public health, 25, 40
Public Health Service Act, 5, 33
public policy, 6
publishing, 16
purpura, 28

R

rash, 52
reactions, 39, 72, 82
reading, 71, 72, 73, 82, 83
reasoning, 70
recognition, 64
recommendations, 6, 27, 33, 34
Reform, 3, 86
regulations, 16, 39, 67, 80, 85
rehabilitation, 49
relief, 65, 69, 84
rent, 22
reporters, 22
requirements, 44, 59, 63, 64, 67, 71, 81, 85
researchers, 35, 38
resolution, 78
response, 23, 83
restrictions, 37, 75
revenue, 18, 19, 37
rights, 61
risk(s), 9, 64, 80, 85
rotavirus, 15, 16, 29, 31, 36, 37
rubella, 13, 28, 30, 35, 37, 40, 75
rules, 2, 6, 34, 35, 77, 85

S

safety, 40, 70, 80, 84, 85
science, 16, 72
scientific publications, 65, 76
scope, 61, 65, 66, 70
securities, 19, 37
seizure, 68, 80
seller, 80
settlements, 16, 24, 27, 34, 64
showing, 6, 33, 78, 82, 86
side effects, vii, 1, 3, 40, 65, 66, 67, 70, 72, 73, 74, 81, 82, 83
signals, 77
skin, 52
smoking, 81
spending, vii, 2, 4, 5, 17, 22
spinal cord, 52
stability, 79
stakeholders, 4, 16, 23, 24, 26, 33
state(s), 36, 68, 70, 71, 75, 76, 77, 78, 79, 80, 81, 84, 85
statute of limitations, 26, 38, 68, 78
statutes, 61, 85
stomach, 51, 52
structure, 66, 71, 72, 73, 74
Supreme Court, 46, 65, 66, 72, 76, 79, 81, 83, 84
suspensions, 35
swelling, 49, 51, 52
swollen glands, 52
symptoms, 53

T

target, 2, 11, 25, 27
target population(s), 27
taxes, 3, 18, 19, 37
technical comments, viii, 2, 27
technological advancement, 75
technological advances, 75
technology, 72
testing, 44, 81
tetanus, 28, 30, 37, 40, 47, 52, 61, 68
thimerosal, 13, 75, 76, 84
time frame, 4, 36
time periods, 12, 47
Tort Law, 85, 86
toxin, 82
tracks, 35
trade, 68
transparency, 24
Treasury, vii, viii, 2, 3, 5, 6, 8, 18, 19, 27, 37, 38
treatment, 53, 80, 82
trust fund, vii, 1, 2, 3, 4, 5, 6, 8, 17, 18, 19, 22, 24, 27, 35, 37, 38, 59
type 1 diabetes, 36

U

U.S. Court of Federal Claims, viii, 2, 3, 4, 10, 11, 19, 22, 40, 51, 59, 61, 76, 77, 84
uniform, 77
United, v, 1, 8, 42, 52, 53, 61, 63, 64, 67, 69, 70, 79, 81
United States, v, 1, 8, 42, 52, 53, 61, 63, 64, 67, 69, 70, 79, 81
updating, 16, 25
USCFC, vii, viii, 2, 3, 4, 6, 7, 8, 9, 10, 12, 18, 19, 21, 22, 27, 33, 34, 35, 36, 37

V

vaccinations, 13, 25, 36, 65, 78
vaccine design, 65, 66, 70, 74, 75, 77
Vaccine Injury Compensation Trust Fund, vii, 2, 4, 6, 8, 17, 19, 24, 35, 59
vaccine injury table, vii, 2, 4, 6, 7, 14, 15, 16, 17, 18, 26, 31, 34, 36, 38
vaccines, vii, viii, 1, 2, 3, 6, 13, 14, 15, 16, 17, 19, 25, 26, 29, 31, 33, 34, 36, 37, 39, 40, 41, 42, 45, 47, 59, 61, 64, 65, 67, 69, 70, 71, 75, 76, 77, 79, 80, 83, 84
vacuum, 75
VICP, vii, viii, 1, 2, 3, 4, 5, 6, 7, 8, 9, 12, 13, 14, 15, 16, 17, 18, 19, 20, 21, 22, 23, 24, 25, 26, 27, 29, 31, 33, 34, 35, 36, 37, 38, 39, 40, 41, 42, 43, 44, 45, 47, 50, 51, 59, 61, 62, 63, 64
viral infection, 28
virus infection, 48
vomiting, 52
vote, 66, 72

W

war, 37
warts, 53
Washington, 33, 37, 51, 83, 84
weakness, 15
websites, 25
whooping cough, 80